# Competing for Customers and Winning with Value

D0731889

# Competing for Customers and Winning with Value

## Breakthrough Strategies for Market Dominance

**R. Eric Reidenbach and Reginald W. Goeke**

ASQ Quality Press
Milwaukee, Wisconsin

American Society for Quality, Quality Press, Milwaukee 53203
© 2006 by ASQ Quality Press
All rights reserved. Published 2006
Printed in the United States of America

12  11  10  09  08  07  06   5  4  3  2  1

### Library of Congress Cataloging-in-Publication Data

Reidenbach, R. Eric.
  Competing for customers and winning with value : breakthrough strategies for
market dominance / R. Eric Reidenbach and Reginald W. Goeke.-- 1st ed.
      p. cm.
  Includes bibliographical references.
  ISBN 0-87389-680-7
  1.  Business planning.  I. Goeke, Reginald W. II. Title.

  HD30.28.R4193 2006
  658.4'012--dc22

                                                                    2005035019

ISBN-13: 978-0-87389-680-1
ISBN-10: 0-87389-680-7

Publisher: William A. Tony
Acquisitions Editor: Annemieke Hytinen
Project Editor: Paul O'Mara
Production Administrator: Randall Benson

ASQ Mission: The American Society for Quality advances individual,
organizational, and community excellence worldwide through learning, quality
improvement, and knowledge exchange.

Attention Bookstores, Wholesalers, Schools, and Corporations: ASQ Quality Press
books, videotapes, audiotapes, and software are available at quantity discounts
with bulk purchases for business, educational, or instructional use. For
information, please contact ASQ Quality Press at 800-248-1946, or write to ASQ
Quality Press, P.O. Box 3005, Milwaukee, WI 53201-3005.

To place orders or to request a free copy of the ASQ Quality Press Publications
Catalog, including ASQ membership information, call 800-248-1946. Visit our
Web site at www.asq.org or http://qualitypress.asq.org.
Printed on acid-free paper

Quality Press
600 N. Plankinton Avenue
Milwaukee, Wisconsin 53203
Call toll free 800-248-1946
Fax 414-272-1734
www.asq.org
http://qualitypress.asq.org
http://standardsgroup.asq.org
E-mail: authors@asq.org

# Contents

*List of Tables and Figures* . . . . . . . . . . . . . . . . . . . . . . . . . *ix*

*Preface* . . . . . . . . . . . . . . . . . . . . . . . . . . . . . . . . . . *xi*

*Introduction* . . . . . . . . . . . . . . . . . . . . . . . . . . . . . . . . *xiii*

**Part I   The Competitive Foundation**
**Chapter 1   Planning for Competition** . . . . . . . . . . . . . . . . **3**
    Corporate-Level Planning . . . . . . . . . . . . . . . . . . . . . . . . 5
    Strategic Business Unit Planning . . . . . . . . . . . . . . . . . 6
    Product/Market-Level Planning . . . . . . . . . . . . . . . . . . . 7

**Chapter 2   The Value Advantage** . . . . . . . . . . . . . . . . . **13**
    What Is Customer Value? . . . . . . . . . . . . . . . . . . . . . . . 13
    Value Properties . . . . . . . . . . . . . . . . . . . . . . . . . . . . . . 16
    Why Value and Not Satisfaction? . . . . . . . . . . . . . . . . . . 18
    What Factors Make Value a Better Strategic Measure? . . . . . 21

**Chapter 3   Growing Market Share with Value: Customer**
                 **Acquisition** . . . . . . . . . . . . . . . . . . . . . . . . **23**
    The Value Model: The Information Platform . . . . . . . . . . 24
    The Competitive Value Matrix: The Strategic Radar Screen . . 26
    Driver-Level Analysis . . . . . . . . . . . . . . . . . . . . . . . . . 28
    Attribute-Level Analysis . . . . . . . . . . . . . . . . . . . . . . . 29
    The Vulnerability Matrix: A Powerful Acquisition Tool . . . . . 31

**Chapter 4  Growing Market Share with Value:**
**Customer Retention** . . . . . . . . . . . . . . . . . . **35**
The Value of Customer Loyalty . . . . . . . . . . . . . . . . 37
Assessing Customer Loyalty . . . . . . . . . . . . . . . . . . 39
Using the Customer Loyalty Matrix for Interventions . . . . . . 42

**Part II  The Competitive Planning Process**
**Chapter 5  Choosing Where to Compete** . . . . . . . . . . . . **49**
Focus, Focus, Focus . . . . . . . . . . . . . . . . . . . . . 50

**Chapter 6  What Is the Organization's Current Value**
**Proposition?** . . . . . . . . . . . . . . . . . . . . . **63**
What Is Your Current Value Proposition? . . . . . . . . . . . 63
Competitive Value Analysis . . . . . . . . . . . . . . . . . . 65
Value Strengths and Weaknesses . . . . . . . . . . . . . . . . 66
Identification of Market Opportunities . . . . . . . . . . . . 70
Customer Acquisition . . . . . . . . . . . . . . . . . . . . . 74
Customer Retention . . . . . . . . . . . . . . . . . . . . . . 76

**Chapter 7  What Does the Organization Want Its**
**Competitive Value Proposition to Be?** . . . . . . . . **81**
Product/Market Objectives . . . . . . . . . . . . . . . . . . 82
Develop a Product/Market Strategy . . . . . . . . . . . . . . 84

**Chapter 8  How Does the Organization Manage Its Value**
**Proposition?** . . . . . . . . . . . . . . . . . . . . . **99**
Marketing Mix Objectives . . . . . . . . . . . . . . . . . . . 99
Product/Market Action Programs . . . . . . . . . . . . . . . 103
Budgets and Forecasts . . . . . . . . . . . . . . . . . . . . 105

**Chapter 9  The Value-Strategy-Process Linkage** . . . . . . . . **109**
Calculate Critical Value Gaps . . . . . . . . . . . . . . . . 111
Identify the Key Value Stream . . . . . . . . . . . . . . . . 112
Constructing the CTQ/Process Matrix . . . . . . . . . . . . . 115
Target Processes for Six Sigma or Lean Projects . . . . . . . 117
Establish Priorities for Lean or Six Sigma Projects . . . . . 119

**Chapter 10  Monitoring Plan Effectiveness** . . . . . . . . . . **123**
Internal Performance Metrics . . . . . . . . . . . . . . . . . 124
Transactional Measures of Customer Value . . . . . . . . . . . 126
Diagnostic Snapshots . . . . . . . . . . . . . . . . . . . . . 132
Alignment of Business Information Systems . . . . . . . . . . 134

**Part III  Competitive Planning Deployment**

**Chapter 11  Fourteen Keys to Successful Deployment** . . . . . **137**
Short-Term Keys to Successful Deployment . . . . . . . . . . . 139
Keys to Success for the Long Haul . . . . . . . . . . . . . . 147

**Chapter 12    Competing for Customers** . . . . . . . . . . . . . . **157**
    What Is the Organization's Current Value Proposition? . . . . . 159
    What Is the Organization's Intended Value Proposition? . . . . 159
    Has the Organization Achieved Its Objectives? . . . . . . . . . 161

**Appendix A    Technical Notes on Value Measurement** . . . . . . **163**
    Attributes/Value Performance Criteria . . . . . . . . . . . . . . 163
    Importance Scores: Stated versus Derived . . . . . . . . . . . 163
    Multicollinearity . . . . . . . . . . . . . . . . . . . . . . . . . 164
    R Squares  . . . . . . . . . . . . . . . . . . . . . . . . . . . . 165
    Model Characteristics  . . . . . . . . . . . . . . . . . . . . . . 165

**Appendix B    Environmental Trend Analysis** . . . . . . . . . . . **167**

**Appendix C    Competitive Market Planning Forms** . . . . . . . **171**
    Product/Market Matrix . . . . . . . . . . . . . . . . . . . . . . 173
    Environmental Scanning . . . . . . . . . . . . . . . . . . . . . 174
    Qualifying Needs of Segment  . . . . . . . . . . . . . . . . . . 175
    Determining Needs of Segment  . . . . . . . . . . . . . . . . . 176
    Market Share and Trends  . . . . . . . . . . . . . . . . . . . . 177
    Value Proposition Assessment  . . . . . . . . . . . . . . . . . 178
    Differential Value Advantage/Disadvantage . . . . . . . . . . . 179
    Market Opportunity Identification . . . . . . . . . . . . . . . . 180
    Strategy and Objectives  . . . . . . . . . . . . . . . . . . . . . 181
    Product/Market Action Programs  . . . . . . . . . . . . . . . . 182
    Budget and Market Forecast . . . . . . . . . . . . . . . . . . . 183

*Glossary*  . . . . . . . . . . . . . . . . . . . . . . . . . . . . . . . . *185*

*References* . . . . . . . . . . . . . . . . . . . . . . . . . . . . . . . . *189*

*Index*  . . . . . . . . . . . . . . . . . . . . . . . . . . . . . . . . . . *191*

# List of Tables and Figures

| | | |
|---|---|---|
| Figure 1.1 | The Context of Competitive Decision Making . . . . . . . . . | 4 |
| Figure 1.2 | Growth Strategies . . . . . . . . . . . . . . . . . . . . . . . | 5 |
| Figure 2.1 | A Comprehensive View of Value . . . . . . . . . . . . . . . | 14 |
| Figure 2.2 | Customer Value Drives Profitability . . . . . . . . . . . . . | 20 |
| Figure 3.1 | Competitive Value Model: Printing Equipment/Large Container Manufacturers . . . . . . . . . . . . . . . . . . . . | 24 |
| Figure 3.2 | Competitive Value Matrix: Printing Equipment/Large Container Manufacturers . . . . . . . . . . . . . . . . . . . . | 27 |
| Table 3.1 | Driver-Level Analysis . . . . . . . . . . . . . . . . . . . . | 28 |
| Table 3.2 | VPC-Level Analysis . . . . . . . . . . . . . . . . . . . . . | 29 |
| Figure 3.3 | Competitive Vulnerability Matrix—Competitor 1 . . . . . . . | 31 |
| Table 3.3 | Quality Driver Analysis—Competitor 1 . . . . . . . . . . . | 33 |
| Figure 4.1 | Customer Value Matrix: Printing Equipment/Large Container Manufacturers . . . . . . . . . . . . . . . . . . . . | 40 |
| Figure 4.2 | The Customer Loyalty Matrix . . . . . . . . . . . . . . . . | 41 |
| Table 4.1 | Recommendation and Switching Intentions by Value Group . . . | 42 |
| Table 4.2 | Quality and Driver Scores by Value Group . . . . . . . . . . | 43 |
| Table 4.3 | Sales Process VPC Ratings for Value Group 4 . . . . . . . . | 44 |
| Figure 4.3 | Value Groups by Distributor Territories . . . . . . . . . . . | 45 |
| Figure 5.1 | Planning Levels and Purposes . . . . . . . . . . . . . . . . | 50 |
| Figure 5.2 | Product/Market Matrix . . . . . . . . . . . . . . . . . . . . | 51 |
| Figure 5.3 | Product/Market Matrix: Plastics Equipment Manufacturer . . | 54 |
| Figure 5.4 | Product/Market Matrix: Heavy-Equipment Dealership . . . . | 56 |
| Table 5.1 | Market Attractiveness . . . . . . . . . . . . . . . . . . . . | 57 |
| Table 5.2 | Ability to Compete . . . . . . . . . . . . . . . . . . . . . . | 58 |
| Figure 5.5 | Market Segment Investment Matrix . . . . . . . . . . . . . . | 59 |
| Figure 5.6 | Heavy-Equipment Dealer's Priorities . . . . . . . . . . . . . | 59 |
| Figure 5.7 | Product/Market Matrix: Financial Services . . . . . . . . . . | 60 |
| Figure 5.8 | Aligning National and Local Competitive Opportunities . . . | 61 |
| Figure 6.1 | Competitive Value Model—Disability Insurance/Large Businesses . . . . . . . . . . . . . . . . . . . . . . . . . . | 64 |

| | | |
|---|---|---|
| Figure 6.2 | Competitive Value Matrix—Disability Insurance/Large Businesses | 66 |
| Table 6.1 | Head-to-Head Driver Analysis | 67 |
| Table 6.2 | Driver VPCs for Disability Insurance | 68 |
| Table 6.3 | Strengths and Weaknesses at the VPC Level | 70 |
| Figure 6.3 | Value Opportunity Identification Matrix | 71 |
| Figure 6.4 | Competitive Value Matrix—Disability Insurance/Large Businesses | 75 |
| Table 6.4 | Competititor Vulnerabilities | 76 |
| Table 6.5 | Quality Driver Performance Ratings—Competitor 3 | 76 |
| Table 6.6 | Quality Driver Performance Ratings—Competitor 5 | 76 |
| Figure 6.5 | Customer Loyalty Matrix—XYZ Company | 77 |
| Table 6.7 | XYZ Performance Ratings by Value Group | 79 |
| Figure 7.1 | Forklifts/Warehouse Value Model—Internal Perspective | 84 |
| Figure 7.2 | Forklifts/Warehouse Value Model—Market Perspective | 85 |
| Figure 7.3 | Forklifts/Warehouse Value Propositions—Internal Perspective | 85 |
| Figure 7.4 | Forklifts/Warehouse Value Propositions—Market Perspective | 86 |
| Figure 7.5 | Competitive Value Matrix—ISP/Residential Users | 87 |
| Table 7.1 | Head-to-Head Driver Analysis—Lift Trucks/Warehouse | 88 |
| Figure 7.6 | Value Opportunity Identification Matrix | 89 |
| Table 7.2 | Head-to-Head VPC Analysis | 91 |
| Figure 7.7 | Simulation at $T_1$ | 92 |
| Figure 7.8 | Simulation at $T_4$ | 94 |
| Figure 7.9 | Customer Loyalty Matrix | 95 |
| Table 7.3 | Value Group Driver Ratings | 96 |
| Figure 8.1 | Marketing Mix Objectives | 101 |
| Table 8.1 | Product/Market Action Program—Service | 104 |
| Table 8.2 | Product/Market Action Program—Sales | 106 |
| Figure 8.2 | Budget and Market Forecast | 107 |
| Figure 9.1 | The Value-Strategy-Process Linkage | 110 |
| Table 9.1 | Calculation of CTQ Gaps | 111 |
| Figure 9.2 | Customer-Focused Value Stream | 112 |
| Table 9.2 | Value Performance Criteria Gaps | 114 |
| Table 9.3 | CTQ/Process Matrix | 116 |
| Figure 9.3 | The Service/Repair Value Stream Map | 118 |
| Table 9.4 | Process Improvement Opportunities | 120 |
| Table 10.1 | Objectives Require Monitoring Metrics | 124 |
| Table 10.2 | Action Programs and Performance Measures | 125 |
| Figure 10.1 | Repair Promise/Delivery Times | 126 |
| Figure 10.2 | Transactional Survey | 128 |
| Figure 10.3 | Survey Linkage to CRM | 130 |
| Figure 10.4 | Menu-Driven Reporting System | 131 |
| Figure 10.5 | Performance Trend Report | 131 |
| Figure 10.6 | Management Dashboard | 132 |
| Figure 10.7 | Electricity/Residential Users Value Model | 133 |
| Table 10.3 | "Routine Transactions" Attributes | 133 |
| Figure 11.1 | Customer Value Linkage to Six Sigma | 150 |
| Figure 11.2 | A Structure in Support of a Strategy | 153 |
| Figure 12.1 | The Context of Competitive Planning | 158 |

# Preface

*C*ompeting for Customers and Winning with Value brings together, for the first time, two very powerful concepts: customer value and competitive planning. Together they create a tool that will generate breakthrough strategies for market dominance.

Value is not a new concept. On the contrary, the concept of value has been around for a long time, but the ability to operationalize that concept into a meaningful tool for business managers has come about much more recently. The previously fashionable metrics of customer satisfaction have proven to be poor predictors of business performance, whereas the linkages between customer value and performance measures such as market share and profitability have been identified and documented. In fact, value has been shown to be one of the best predictors of market share and customer loyalty available. It is only natural, then, that developing a system to harness value as a competitive weapon is an essential next step. This is the objective of *Competing for Customers*.

The second concept that *Competing with Customers* brings to the table is a competitive planning template that enables organizations to actually harness their value-creation and delivery systems to enhance their market performance. It is a planning system that focuses at the level where the organization makes money: selling products or services to people in specific markets or market segments.

Every business organization has plans for growth—whether these are formal or informal, well-documented or intuitive. This type of planning is typically done at the highest levels of the organization, and usually does not and cannot address the questions of *where* and *how* the organization should compete in order to win and retain customers. And when competitive planning at the more granular level does take place, there is frequently a disconnection between these planning levels, with the result that the organization plows without a rudder through the competitive waters, unable to navigate the demanding currents of the marketplace. *Competing for Customers* provides the framework for bringing the multiple levels of planning into alignment, and for addressing very specifically the question, "How do we compete?"

Organizations have the power to choose *where* they compete and *how* they compete. The competitive arena is a product/market—a market or market segment that buys specific products or services. This is where competitive planning takes place. It focuses on answering a series of very specific questions using the metrics of customer value. It accommodates the shifting complexities of a constantly changing marketplace by creating the necessary focus to understand how competitors compete.

Within each product/market in which the organization chooses to compete, the first question is "What is the organization's competitive value proposition?" How do buyers within the product/market define the value they seek, and how do they perceive the value our organization provides relative to that of the competition? Failing to answer these two questions or, worse, not asking them in the first place, puts the organization at a severe competitive disadvantage.

Once the organization understands its competitive value proposition it has to ask "Is this the value proposition that we want?" If the organization's value proposition is undifferentiated from its competitors, it is offering buyers no compelling reason to buy its products. This results in stagnating share positions and mediocre profits. If its actual value proposition is inferior to its competitors, then it can expect declining share positions and lower profits.

Understanding the value gaps between an organization and its competitors, along with the potential value-enhancing opportunities those present, raises the question "How does the organization manage its competitive value proposition in order to either close the value gap with leading competitors or widen it in order to establish undisputed leadership?" *Competing for Customers* provides a blueprint for effectively managing the organization's value proposition by specifying clear objectives supported by a clear and focused strategy.

Finally, the organization has to monitor its competitive value proposition. The organization's value proposition is an important asset providing a compelling reason to do business with the organization. It requires continuous management. Just as an organization manages its inventories, distribution system, or pricing strategies, so too must it manage its value proposition. Failure to do so means that the organization is leaving this critically important asset to the whims of its competitors.

*Competing for Customers and Winning with Value* provides the reader with a clear blueprint for crafting breakthrough, value-added strategies to dominate those product/markets that the organization targets. For many readers it will challenge the way they look at their competition, their markets, and their industries. Competition will never look the same.

# Introduction

Elementary economics would tell you that every business firm seeks to identify and occupy a position that is somehow unique from that of its competitors. This is the very essence of competition. Uniqueness creates a compelling selling proposition and an opportunity to increase the firm's share of the market as long as the uniqueness is something that is valued by the market. In the past, and to a large extent even today, this uniqueness has been based on product differences such as those created and enjoyed by Microsoft. Distribution differences, such as those that have powered the Caterpillar engine, are another form of differentiation. Image differences have been a powerful tool employed by companies such as Mercedes and Lexus. Price differences are yet another type of differentiation, perhaps no better employed than by Wal-Mart, Costco, and Yugo. Outstanding firms are constantly seeking newer and better ways to differentiate themselves from their competitors.

All firms compete. Some are better at it than are others. Less innovative firms that lack the ability and capacity to effectively differentiate can only challenge the leaders at best, or are destined to follow. Some industries, to their current detriment, have managed themselves into a commodity situation in which differentiation is no longer possible.

The retail banking industry had, in response to the dying Savings and Loan (S&L) industry, bet the mortgage on a price competition, in which the belief was that the only way banks could woo customers from the S&Ls was to cut their fees and prices. In the face of the dubious S&L strategy of losing a dollar on every transaction and making it up in volume, bank managements panicked and began cutting prices. In fact, this price cutting evolved into strategies of giving products and services away for free. The current result is that many banks have turned themselves into "kernels of corn" or "hog bellies" in the eyes of their markets. There is little if any differentiation among banks. They are, in fact, commodities offering commodity products and services. To quote Gertrude Stein, "A bank is a bank is a bank." Unfortunately, as any marketer worth his or her salt will tell you, there need be no such thing as a commodity. Just ask Orville Redenbacher or Sam Purdue.

Banks are not alone. The U.S. airline industry has flown into significant turbulence as the flying public has learned that it can endure a cramped, stressful, and all-around uncomfortable traveling experience on any airline. It doesn't matter if it's Delta, United, U.S. Airways, or Continental. All are the same. The issue thus becomes one of how to lure customers. Perhaps through improved service, on-time arrivals, or comfortable seating? No—reduced prices are the method of choice. Now you can fly in the same cramped, stressful, and all-around uncomfortable airlines at a cheaper price. The futility of such an approach is obvious.

Telecom has also found that the conventional wisdom of trying to differentiate a dial tone is a difficult process. Ignoring the host of attendant services and support that customers want, telecom companies dialed down their prices in an attempt to lure customers from one carrier to another.

A second law of economics points to the nature of competition and how it forces firms to differentiate. When Henry Ford began the mass production and mass marketing of his automobile his strategy was simple—"Give them any color car that they want as long as it's black." Ford saw the U.S. automobile buyer market as homogeneous. Thus entered the competition. Now the challenge was how to offer the U.S. auto buyer a compelling reason to buy new products instead of Ford's car. The answer, of course, was to provide something different—a different color, style, name, and so forth. As more and more companies entered the auto market, the greater became the need to differentiate.

Competition forces differentiation, and in the face of a growing and intensive global competition, firms must learn how to compete effectively. They must better learn how to create and sustain a differential advantage or they will relegate themselves to the status of a mere challenger or, worse, a follower.

The competition for a differential advantage, as indicated, has taken many forms. Neutralization of these advantages has become significantly easier, making the advantage less sustainable. Price advantages have always been recognized as the easiest and quickest to be neutralized. However, technology and its availability to all types of businesses has made it easier to neutralize product, distribution, and even image advantages.

Organizations are beginning to understand how value—customer value—is a powerful differentiator providing the basis for a differential value advantage highly linked to increased market share and profitability. It is a differential advantage less susceptible to neutralization.

Value forces the organization to critically examine and understand the all-important interaction among the enterprise's quality offering, its pricing policies, and its brand/corporate image. The key to the successful deployment of a value strategy is understanding how targeted customers define quality and how to operationalize the quality definition.

What is quality? Is it simply a better product or service? Or does it involve how the product is delivered and serviced? How do the different quality components interact and combine with price to provide superior value? How does the enterprise manage its competitive value proposition to achieve targeted performance goals? These are critical questions, the answers to which drive successful organizational initiatives.

The process of creating a differential advantage has always been somewhat more "magic" than science—magic in the sense that it is random and not a systematic outcome of a deliberate and disciplined approach. This is easily substantiated by noting the number of followers or challengers relative to true market leaders. Clearly, there are more followers than there are leaders. Unfortunately, too many organizations treat the competition for customers as an unsystematic, agenda-driven process often directed by corporate lore and the individual with the loudest voice.

This is the challenge facing many organizations today. How does an organization create and deploy a process that makes the organization an effective machine for attracting new customers and holding onto current customers? How does a business enterprise hardwire a competitive differentiation process into its culture and its way of doing things? Can a challenger or a follower become a leader? Can a process of differentiation be learned and incorporated into enterprise management?

As noted earlier, all firms compete, but not all firms compete effectively. Many firms stumble over the first question in effective competition—where do you compete? Do you compete across all market segments and all product lines? The idea that a business enterprise can and should be all things to everybody has long passed, but the myth, in practice, still lingers.

This book is about competition—effective competition—for customers. There is a systematic and disciplined approach, a step-by-step process, for creating and sustaining a differential advantage that can be deployed throughout the different functional and operational areas of the organization. It is a systematic process designed to remove the randomness of crafting effective competitive strategy. It is a process that is arguably more important than Six Sigma or lean initiatives, and learning how to use this process will make Six Sigma, lean, or any other planning program even more powerful.

*Competing for Customers* is broken down into three major parts. Part I focuses on issues of value and its relationship to market performance. The first part includes chapters 1 through 4 and begins with understanding the context and roles of the different aspects of corporate strategy. These roles are often mixed up, resulting in competitive confusion. The introduction focuses on the context of competition and discusses three issues of competition: (1) how the organization grows, (2) where it competes, and (3) how the organization competes. The first issue is a higher-level question that corporate-level types must decide. The second and third issues are answered at the SBU (strategic business unit) or division level. The latter are the two critical components of competition.

Chapter 2 takes an in-depth look at a powerful concept and how it propels sustainable advantages: customer value. Customer value provides both the conceptual basis for creating and sustaining a differential competitive advantage while at the same time providing the operational tools for deploying a value-driven competitive strategy. In recent years customer satisfaction has provided the strategic measure employed by many organizations. Unfortunately, customer satisfaction has proven incapable of providing the critical information platform that has actionable linkages to factors such as market share, return on sales, or top-line revenue.

Chapter 3 discusses four value tools that enable the enterprise to understand value and deploy this understanding to achieve a superior competitive value proposition. These tools focus on both the acquisition of new customers and the retention of current customers. Both are key to increasing profitable market share.

The fourth chapter provides a tool for answering the question "Where do we compete?" The reader is introduced to the product/market matrix. By aligning the two key factors for revenue generation—products and customers—the product/market matrix provides a basis for identifying key opportunities for competition. Instead of trying to be everything to everyone, the product/market matrix permits the sorting of different opportunities in terms of their greatest economic and strategic potential for the organization. These are the competitive battlegrounds for investment.

Chapters 5 through 10 constitute the second part of the book. Part II is dedicated to the explanation and illustration of how the competitive planning process is operationalized. Chapter 5 begins a discussion that examines the issue of "How do we compete?" Understanding the organization's current value proposition is a key to effective competition. Every organization has a value proposition, arguably one of the firm's most important assets. How to improve or leverage the firm's value proposition is a critical decision.

The second chapter in the "How do we compete?" sequence (Chapter 6) focuses on the question of "What do we want our value proposition to be?" Are we to lead, challenge, follow, or niche? These are the four options facing the firm.

Chapter 7 looks at the question "How do we manage our value proposition?" What do we need to do to lead, to challenge, to follow, or to niche? What is necessary to pull the organization's resources together to compete effectively?

Chapter 8 focuses on the key processes that actually deliver the enterprise's value offering. These processes are the ones that determine how customers define the organization's competitive value proposition.

A systematic approach for linking the organization's competitive strategy to key process improvements is detailed in Chapter 9. Many organizations already use the tools of lean or Six Sigma for cost or defect reductions. The challenge for those organizations is to align their process improvement initiatives with their competitive strategy. This chapter describes how to achieve that alignment, capitalizing on the identification of market-defined critical-to-quality factors (CTQs) and linking those to key value streams and business processes.

Chapter 10 is devoted to a discussion of how to monitor plan effectiveness. Is the plan accomplishing what it is intended to accomplish? If not, where is it deviating and why is it deviating from its intended objective? This is critical to know and understand.

The final and third part of the book includes chapters 11 and 12, which focus on how the organization can implement a competitive planning process and provide a final checklist for the process. Chapter 11 examines deployment and implementation issues and suggests ways in which the enterprise can develop an effective competitive planning process.

Finally, Chapter 12 provides a summary of key points to keep in mind regarding the competitive planning process. These key points are linked to the specific chapters in which they are discussed so that the reader can revisit the specific information dedicated to their explication.

Appendix A provides further technical information on value measurement, and Appendix B discusses environmental scanning more thoroughly. Appendix C provides blank versions of the matrices and forms used throughout the text for reader-specific use.

# Part I:
# The Competitive Foundation

## Chapter 1
Planning for Competition

## Chapter 2
The Value Advantage

## Chapter 3
Growing Market Share with Value: Customer Acquisition

## Chapter 4
Growing Market Share with Value: Customer Retention

# 1

# Planning for Competition

Most businesspeople would agree that competing effectively requires a plan. No competent general would willingly go into battle without a carefully developed plan of attack, and no competent organization should deploy for competitive action without a good plan for winning. But a plan for winning against the competition is not one of those documents that management develops once every three to five years, then pulls off the shelf periodically to check on progress. Rather, effective competitive planning is focused on a very specific battlefield, against very specific competitive enemies, and relies upon dynamic feedback from the marketplace about the relative strengths and weaknesses of competitive offerings. The tools for effective competitive planning must build upon the specific criteria used by the marketplace to make those comparative evaluations.

In our experience working with a vast array of different types of organizations, there is much confusion regarding what plans are, who should craft them, and what their focus should be. The 1960s and 1970s saw the rise of strategic planning as an almost mystical and Delphic process conducted by a few enlightened individuals. The 1980s and 1990s debunked the myth of strategic planning and made it a much more operational and less conceptual process. But competitive planning is not the same as strategic planning. It is much more granular, and while strategic planning may provide a 50,000-foot view, competitive planning reflects the dynamics of a ground-level perspective. After all, it is at this level that the real competition for customers takes place.

One possible reason for all the confusion about planning is that it serves different purposes at different levels within an organization. Figure 1.1 shows the context in which competitive planning actually takes place. There are essentially three levels at which planning takes place within any organization: the corporate level, the division or business-unit level, and the product/market level. Small enterprises may have only one strategic business unit (SBU), but the purposes of corporate and business-unit planning must still be addressed separately. Competitive planning is what takes place at the product/market level.

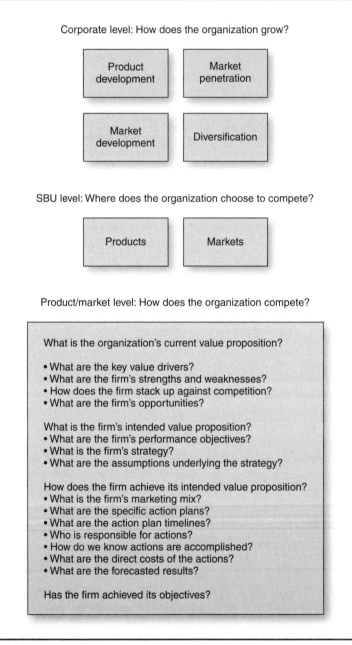

Corporate level: How does the organization grow?

| | |
|---|---|
| Product development | Market penetration |
| Market development | Diversification |

SBU level: Where does the organization choose to compete?

| | |
|---|---|
| Products | Markets |

Product/market level: How does the organization compete?

What is the organization's current value proposition?

• What are the key value drivers?
• What are the firm's strengths and weaknesses?
• How does the firm stack up against competition?
• What are the firm's opportunities?

What is the firm's intended value proposition?
• What are the firm's performance objectives?
• What is the firm's strategy?
• What are the assumptions underlying the strategy?

How does the firm achieve its intended value proposition?
• What is the firm's marketing mix?
• What are the specific action plans?
• What are the action plan timelines?
• Who is responsible for actions?
• How do we know actions are accomplished?
• What are the direct costs of the actions?
• What are the forecasted results?

Has the firm achieved its objectives?

**Figure 1.1**  The context of competitive decision making.

Again, our experience indicates that in many organizations these planning levels are disconnected from one another. The corporate-level plans, designed to address *how the organization will grow,* are insufficient to direct organizations in *how they will compete.* That is not their purpose. They are far too global and lack the necessary focus. The SBU-level plans identify *where* to compete but not *how* to compete. They can't. But by bringing into focus where the organization *chooses* to compete, competitive plans can be developed that focus on *how to compete*. The bridging function of SBU planning melds the strategic with the competitive, making the organization a much more effective competitor.

# CORPORATE-LEVEL PLANNING

Corporate-level planning addresses a specific question: *How does the organization grow?* This is the level of planning that has attracted much attention and has been addressed by Porter (1985) and Ansoff (1957), among other corporate-level strategic thinkers. The "How does the organization grow?" question essentially has four answers. These are shown in Figure 1.2.

*Market penetration* occurs when the organization increases its selling efforts to move more of its current product into the markets that it currently serves. This is done on a virtually daily basis as competitors attempt to increase their current market shares. The limit to this strategy as a growth strategy is, of course, market saturation.

*Product development* reflects a strategy of introducing new products into current markets. This is a common growth strategy, and arguably one of the more risk laden because of the often large investment in the new product and the relative uncertainty of its acceptance. Companies that add line extensions as well as radically new products are examples of this strategy. Hybrid cars, digital cameras, and photo phones are some examples of introducing new products into markets of current users.

*Market development* is a growth strategy in which current products are offered in new markets. McDonald's or Disney's expansion into Europe, as well as Caterpillar's move into China, are examples of a market development strategy. *Diversification* directs organizational growth by offering new products to new markets. Diversification often involves the acquisition of

|  | Current products | New products |
|---|---|---|
| **Current markets** | Market penetration | Product development |
| **New markets** | Market development | Diversification |

**Figure 1.2**   Growth strategies.

one company by another or the merger of two companies offering different products to different markets.

Two other growth options are occasionally utilized, albeit less frequently: *vertical integration,* either backward or forward, and *horizontal integration.* Backward integration occurs, for example, when a retailer chooses to grow by providing its own manufacturing capabilities, whereas forward integration might be a growth strategy for a manufacturer taking over its distribution network. Horizontal integration occurs when a company grows by merging with or acquiring competitors.

These types of growth strategies are high-level strategies directing how an organization, at the macro level, will grow. It is very common to see organizations adopt several of these growth strategies at the same time, to be deployed in different areas of their operations. Although this level of planning provides the generic framework for competitive market planning, it does not constitute competitive planning in and of itself. The effectiveness of a corporation's growth strategy(ies) will impact the number and types of business units that make up that corporation.

## STRATEGIC BUSINESS UNIT PLANNING

Planning at the strategic business unit or division level focuses on the question: *Where will we compete?* Because of the size and specialization of different organizations, many are too diverse to have all of their operations function within a single structure. To make management more focused and effective, these organizations subdivide their operations into smaller units called strategic business units or divisions. Typically an SBU exhibits the following characteristics:

1. It has its own business mission

2. It is made up of related products and services

3. It has its own set of competitors

4. It has its own management

5. Planning can take place independently of other business units

One common mistake is to confuse functional areas with SBUs. Many businesses provide a product of one sort or another that requires periodic servicing and consumable parts. Over time, the functional areas of new sales, used sales, rentals, parts, and service take on a structural significance all their own, and many companies make the mistake of treating these functional areas as SBUs. For example, when companies define used sales and new sales as business units, they frequently find that their business units are competing with one another for the same customers, thus driving down overall profits and confusing customers.

Another mistake made by some organizations is to ignore the concept of business units and attempt to take a single approach to competitive planning across all business units. Competitive planning that attempts to take place across all business units is doomed to fail. These plans are generally to broad and too confusing to be deployed with any effectiveness. Experience in the financial services industry points out that many financial services institutions, such as commercial banks, fail to take the idea of business units into consideration and hence their plans are very conceptual and lack clear direction for deployment. This is a cardinal sin in the competitive arena and is one of the principal reasons that plans that are crafted and deployed do not accomplish what they are intended to accomplish—they can't function properly because they lack the necessary detail and focus to be actionable. Ineffective competitive efforts typically flow from a lack of good planning or a lack of any type of planning.

At the SBU level the operant question is: *Where does the business unit focus its attention to accomplish its need for growth?* The complete answer to this question is offered in Chapter 5, but it is important to note at this point that the SBU needs to look at the two elements that drive revenue generation: its product lines and the markets that buy them. Which product lines marketed to which customers should be the focus of attention within the business unit? Not all product lines have the same margins or returns and not all market segments are worth investing in. This means that there are multiple business opportunities that must be prioritized. The SBU probably does not want to focus on selling low-margin products to small or low-growth market segments. It does not have to be all things to all people. It has to choose, based upon specific strategic criteria, which product/markets on which to focus.

A final mistake made by some organizations is to confuse the purposes for planning at the corporate and business-unit levels. Business-unit managers have a constrained set of market segments to which they bring a limited set of products. The planning responsibility of the SBU manager is to determine which intersections of products and markets constitute viable business opportunities, and to establish priorities for the investment of limited resources. This is a critical responsibility because without this focus on strategically important product/markets, truly effective competitive planning simply cannot occur. The organization is done a tremendous disservice if that SBU manager is distracted by the broader question of "How do we grow?" as a corporation, with all that entails. We have witnessed one such case in which the distraction was so crippling that the organization was never able to engage in effective competitive market planning at the appropriate level.

# PRODUCT/MARKET-LEVEL PLANNING

Once specific product/markets are identified they become the focus of competition. They are the designated battlegrounds where the organization will deploy its resources in an effort to acquire and retain customers at the expense of its competition. A key point is that the organization has chosen to compete within these arenas and is not forced to do so. This is an overt decision on the part of management based on their estimate of potential returns to the organization. The question that has to be answered at this level is *How does the organization compete?* The decision as to where the competition will take place has been decided; now it's time to decide how the organization will effectively compete.

This is where profitable market share is actually won or lost. Each product/market will have its own set of competitors. For example, going back to our banking situation, banks offer home loans, auto loans, brokerage services, credit cards. Looking at just credit cards, banks compete against other banks, brokers that offer credit cards, auto companies (GM), retailers (Sears), and telecommunication companies (AT&T), among others. These competitors are different from those that occupy the home loan competitive set or the brokerage set. Each competitive set brings certain capabilities to the market that must be taken into account if the organization is going to be an effective competitor.

There are a series of questions that must be answered at this level:

1. *What is the organization's current value proposition?* Competitive strategies involve determining the basis of customer or client decision making. Generally, these are based on some combination of quality, reputation, and cost. And the interaction of these criteria is the very essence of value. Competitive market planning therefore must focus on customer value because customer value is also the strongest leading indicator of market share (Gale, 1944). Value is the vehicle for building an organization's profitable share by acquiring new customers who seek outstanding value while retaining current customers who are happy with the value they are receiving. Every organization has an existing value proposition. It is defined by how the market evaluates the interaction of the quality of the organization's offering, its image, and the price that it charges for the offering relative to the value of competitive offerings. It is not uncommon to find that many organizations are ignorant or unsure of their competitive value proposition, which is analogous to ignoring their inventory management or their very "bricks and mortar." This typically happens because those organizations lack the specific value tools to properly understand their competitive value proposition. The organization's competitive value proposition is an incredibly important asset that is often mismanaged, or not managed at all. It communicates to the market what customers can expect in terms of the quality of the organization's product or service offering and the cost of this offering to them. It tells customers whether an enterprise's offering is "worth it" or whether it is just another ho-hum, run-of-the-mill offering they can get anywhere. If an organization's value proposition is weak, it signals to customers that they will not get a good deal buying it or that the purchase of the

product or service is not worth it. This concept will be discussed in greater detail in Chapter 2.

To answer this question the organization has to understand how the market segment buying a specific product line defines value. What are the key value drivers? Based on this information, how well does the organization perform on these drivers? How does the organization stack up against competitors on the performance of these drivers? Based on the competitive value analysis, what are the key value opportunities facing the organization? Each product/market will have its own evaluation of an organization's competitive value proposition.

It might be useful to ask how your targeted markets evaluate the product and/or service offering of your organization. Do you know what your value proposition is? Do your colleagues? A useful exercise is to get your management team to identify what they think your competitive value proposition is, and then to actually go out and measure it. To the extent that the mental models of your management match up with the mental model of the market, your organization will be a much more effective competitor. A gap between the two mental models signals a need to get in better touch with your customers. Failure to do so renders competitive efforts less than effective.

It should be clear by now that the answer to these questions, and ultimately the effectiveness of your competitive efforts, will be a function of high-quality, market-based information. It is not possible to compete effectively in the absence of quality information about the market segments you are targeting and the competitors against which you compete. Yet this is exactly why there are so many ineffective competitors. Organizations that lack quality information about both their targeted segments and their competitors render competitive efforts less than effective.

Traditional market research does not provide the kind of information on which to craft effective competitive plans. Traditional market research typically provides a report card, usually focusing only on your company's performance, thereby making the results useless for developing effective competitive plans. Traditional market research can usually, at best, serve as a tactical tool, enabling the organization to react to individual situations at specific moments in time. What is needed is a strategic measure, one that has linkage to important business performance measures such as market share, top-line revenue, or return on investment. This will be further discussed in Chapters 3 and 4.

2. *What is the organization's intended value proposition?* This is another choice facing every organization. Outstanding value competitors are typically the market share leaders. Their value offering is superior to that of their competition and provides an overwhelming buying proposition. They also have the most loyal customer base with high levels of repurchasing, recommendation, and tolerance for price increases. They are less sensitive to competitive intrusion and represent an annuity to the organization.

The organization chooses the nature and character of its competitive value proposition. To do so it has to be able to answer a series of questions, beginning with: What are the firm's specific performance objectives? What increase in market share does it seek? What increase in top-line revenue does it seek? What increase in its value performance does it want? What combination of its marketing mix does it need to accomplish the performance objectives? What has to be done with its product or service lines, its promotion activities, its distribution policies, or its pricing programs? This final question notes the four elements that all organizations have control over; assembling them to accomplish the specified performance objectives is critical.

The firm must also identify its strategy. This will be discussed in much greater detail in Chapter 8. At this point it is sufficient to note that there are only four basic strategic positions:

1. To lead

2. To challenge

3. To follow

4. To niche

The appropriate strategic position within any targeted product/market will be a function of your existing competitive value proposition, who the value leader is, and the size of the value gap between the leader and your organization, or between your organization and lesser value competitors. The elements that will comprise your strategy will be a function of your existing value opportunities vis-à-vis key competitors.

Finally, it is important to articulate the assumptions that underlie the strategy. These are typically environmental in nature and the organization has little, if any, control over such assumptions. Technological changes, competitive changes, legal/political changes, and sociocultural changes can affect any organization and its strategic intent. The competitive plan should, of course, reflect trends and potential changes in any of these factors.

3. *How does the organization achieve the intended value proposition?* What factors regarding the product, its price, and how it's distributed and promoted need to be modified or developed? What are the specific action plans necessary to deploy the specific marketing mix objectives to achieve the broader strategy? When will these actions be accomplished? How do we know that they have been accomplished? Who is responsible for accomplishing them? What are the direct costs of each action? What are the forecasted results of the plan? What is the plan contribution (the difference between the forecasts and the direct costs)? When does the plan produce profitable results (year one, year two, and so on)?

Here is where the plan provides the translation from concept to reality. It provides a clear and detailed roadmap to accomplish the organization's objectives. As such it is a living document, one that has to be reviewed and assessed on a scheduled periodic basis. A common lament of members of planning teams is that too often plans are conceived, crafted, and stuck in a drawer—never to be revisited until the end of the year, which is usually too late to do anything.

> 4. *Has the organization achieved its objectives?* Or perhaps better stated, *Is the organization on track to achieve its objectives?* This involves not only the monitoring from an accounting point of view of those objectives such as top-line revenue growth, but also setting up a tracking system designed to monitor progress toward the intended value proposition and/or to identify if the organization is off track. The monitoring system should be related to the value drivers identified in the first part of the planning process. The organization's competitive value proposition is based on its performance on these drivers. These are the drivers that the product/market has identified as critical in their definitions of value. The greater the performance on the drivers, the better the value proposition score. To make this system operant requires a solid information platform. This information platform provides the strategic foundation for the development and deployment of competitive plans. The sturdier the platform, the better and more powerful the competitive plans. It all begins with reliable and valid information.

Earlier, it was noted that typical market research is not sufficient for driving a high-quality competitive initiative. The information generated from most marketing research efforts lacks evidence of reliability and validity. In fact, most research of this type is incapable of making the kinds of assessments required to evaluate the reliability and validity of the information. To understand the organization's current value proposition requires more than just asking customers to rate the value of a given product or service. It requires understanding how customers define value, the drivers of value and what constitutes these drivers, and how these drivers interact with price and the organization's image. This is where the organization gains the kind of actionability that supports high-quality competitive efforts.

It is not uncommon to find organizations attempting to develop competitive plans without any competitive information whatsoever. Instead they rely on opinions of sales or marketing people. This is analogous to a general attempting to engage an enemy without having any understanding of the enemy's strength, weaknesses, deployment, the configuration of the battlefield, or its weaponry. In other words, planning without good information is a sure-fire, General George Armstrong Custer–type of recipe for suicide or, in the business context, failure.

# 2

# The Value Advantage

Why should you be more concerned about customer value than customer satisfaction? What does value provide that satisfaction does not? If your organization is using customer satisfaction studies, why should you switch to customer value studies? These are three important questions that will be addressed in this Chapter. First, some background on customer value will be covered—what it is, some basic value properties, and why it provides a better understanding of customer buying dynamics than does satisfaction.

## WHAT IS CUSTOMER VALUE?

The concept of customer value is not new. It is the essence of Adam Smith's 1776 treatise on economics and exchange. For our purposes, *value is the relationship between the quality of a product or service, brand/corporate image, and the price that the customer pays to acquire that product or service.*

As shown in Figure 2.1, value is a function of quality, image, and price. Perhaps the most complex element of value resides within the quality component. Though it is inviting to reduce the concept of quality to simply the literal quality of the product or service, that would be extremely shortsighted and would mislead your competitive planning activities. If you ask customers how they define quality relative to a product, many will certainly mention such product elements as reliability, durability, and specific features. If you were to ask customers about quality relative to a service, such as health insurance or banking, they might also mention such things as process efficiency and effectiveness. In either case, however, they will also tell you that such issues as installation, problem resolution, service inquiries, product repairs, and customer service influence their perception and evaluation of quality as well. Probe a little more and they will talk about branches, dealerships, or brokers—the sales experience, the ability of the dealer to solve problems, and other factors related to the firm's channel system. The point is that many

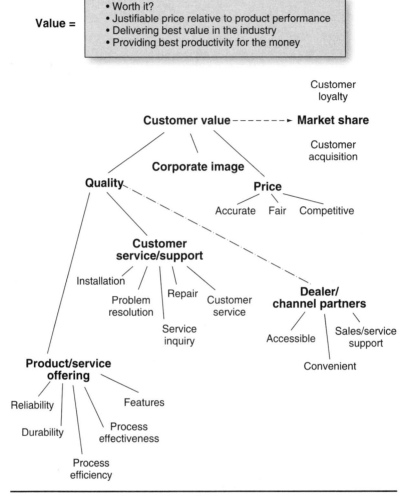

**Figure 2.1** A comprehensive view of value.

firms stop short in their understanding of customer quality by focusing solely on the literal product elements. Customer definitions and perceptions of quality typically extend well beyond the literal quality of a product.

Brand and/or corporate image is also part of the value equation. The impact of image varies from industry to industry. For example, utilities and commercial banks typically have a strong image component that might be described as a social responsibility component, and another image component that speaks to their stability and consistency as a provider of services. Other firms, in high-tech industries for example, will have an image that is more associated with innovation and invention. The main idea is that image has a direct impact on value and represents a part of the equation that must be managed.

Finally, price—or rather the evaluation of price, not specific price points—is the final piece of value. What is important about price is whether customers feel that the price is competitive or fair. This is an evaluation of the firm's price *relative to the prices offered by other competitors.* Part of this price factor may include the trade-in value, discounts, rebates, or other conditions that might impact the evaluation of price.

The calculation of value is something that all customers do, whether buying cheese, cars, vacations, hydraulic excavators, telecom services, or any other product or service. Customers assess the quality of what they think they will get relative to the price they must pay to get it, and determine whether the proposed purchase will be "worth it."

Once the calculation is made and verified by the purchase, the customer has learned about the value of a brand or service. The customer will continue to buy based on the ability of the brand or service to continue to supply the original, or even greater, value. This is the challenge to many suppliers—to maintain and improve their competitive value offering. Failure to do so impels buyers to shop elsewhere and to recalculate the value from alternative suppliers. This explains why and how many suppliers who were once premier suppliers have fallen into the ranks of the "also-rans." They ignored their value proposition and either let quality slip or failed to understand the changes in competitive quality that were showing up in the marketplace.

Some examples might help to clarify this relationship. Suppose you are going to purchase an automobile. As a buyer you will perhaps narrow the competitive set to one or two manufacturers, or manufacturer lines, and even whittle the options down to a sports car or SUV or some other model. Once you have decided on the type as well as the make, you begin assessing the offers of the different dealers carrying those vehicles. What are the factors that you use to evaluate the different offerings? Clearly, there are product considerations such as styling, comfort, ease of operation, power, mileage, accessories (stereo equipment, navigational equipment), and so on. In addition, you may consider dealer-specific attributes such as dealer reputation for honesty, service, parts supply, and the like. Image factors may also come into play. And, of course, you will factor in the price, either in terms of the overall cost of the car or monthly payments (a function of dealer or manufacturer financing options). Once you have gathered all of this information you engage in a cognitive calculation that factors in all of the quality components relative to the price. The winner will be the car and dealer that offers you the "best deal." This is the very essence of value.

Here's another example. You hear about a new restaurant and want to give it a try. After your meal you evaluate your dining experience. To do this you think back on the things that were important to you, such as the atmosphere, the service, the quality of the food, the quantity of the food, and the price. Some of these things will be more important than others, so you will factor these differences into your evaluation. At the end of this assessment you will decide whether or not your dinner was worth the price you paid for it. You will determine the value of the dining experience. Even more important to the owner of the restaurant, your evaluation of that value will determine the probability of you returning to the restaurant. The greater the value, the greater will be the probability of a return visit. Also, the greater the value, the greater the likelihood you will recommend the restaurant to friends.

# VALUE PROPERTIES

There are three important properties of value that aid in its management. A discussion of each follows.

### Value Is Relative

First, *value is relative*. Every product or service offering has a level of value associated with it. You may or may not know how the value of your product stacks up to that of your competitors; but rest assured, your customers and your competitors customers know. They have gone through the cognitive calculations and have made their evaluations. Value is a measure much like return on assets (ROA) or return on investment (ROI). What is a good ROA or ROI? It depends on the industry and who you are comparing it to. This is the relative aspect of customer value.

In this sense it might be better to describe value as competitive. Every company has a competitive value proposition. This is the market's determination of the value that your organization offers relative to that of your competitors. It is as important an asset as your inventories, your distribution system, or any other asset. It provides the compelling buying reason for customers to purchase your product or service and it provides the basic reason why customers stay loyal to your brands, products, and services. Too many organizations fail to actually manage their competitive value proposition, with the result that it is being managed by their competitors. This reflects both the relativity and the competitiveness of customer value.

### Value Is Product and Market Specific

Second, customer *value is product and market specific*. Consider, first, those aspects of value that are product specific. The market's definition of value depends on what product category or service type you are talking about. Clearly, the definition of value will differ whether you are talking about trucks for hauling coal at an open-pit mine site or tractors for plowing land on a farm. Similarly, markets will define value differently for meats and cereals at the local grocery, and for financial planning versus checking account services at the local bank. These contrasting examples may seem self-evident, but it's a continual surprise to observe how many different organizations ask customers to rate their performance across a variety of products or services, then lump these ratings together into a single "report card." This lack of specificity makes effective competitive planning impossible.

With respect to markets, different markets and market segments will also define value differently from one another. Adults buying clothes will define value differently than teenagers. A buyer of electricity from a large industrial organization will define value differently than a buyer from a small service firm. An Australian miner operating under different geological conditions than his or her American counterpart will probably differently define the value he or she wants in a hydraulic excavator. The failure of your measurement system to explicitly account for those differences would make the resulting information less useful for competitive market planning.

In order to manage value effectively, then, it's important to recognize that competitive strategies developed for one market and product line will necessarily be somewhat different than competitive strategies for another group of customers and products. And, in order for those differences to emerge, the tools used to measure market definitions and perceptions of value must be focused on those products and markets most important to your organization's growth. The manner in which to do this will be addressed more fully in Chapter 5, but it's important to have these differences in mind as you consider what type of information to collect and how to analyze that information in order to not obscure those differences.

This type of focus on important products and markets brings with it additional advantages that make competitive market plans highly actionable. Each market segment buying a particular product line becomes a unique competitive arena with its own set of competitors, constraints, and, of course, value definitions. The better an organization understands this competitive arena, the more effective it is in competing for customers within that arena.

## Value Is Learned

Third, *value is learned.* Suppliers actually teach their markets about the value they can expect from the purchase of their product or service offering, and customers do, in fact, learn. The essence of an enterprise's value is contained within its collective competitive value propositions. Every enterprise has a competitive value proposition(s), whether or not it is the intended one. The learning effect of value is perhaps best seen in the actions of companies moving from a regulated environment to an unregulated one. For example, for a long time commercial banks provided customers with a service that was protected. During this time they were telling their customers that the level of value they provided was the level of value that could be expected from providers within their industry. When deregulation let other competitors into their once-protected franchise, customers were exposed to companies such as AT&T, Merrill Lynch, GM, and others that were able to provide superior quality at an even better price. The result was an erosion of financial share for the commercial banking industry as competitors were able to intrude successfully into the once protected markets of commercial banking. Customers were quick to recognize the superior value proposition of these new competitors.

The American auto industry experienced a similar situation once Japanese cars were able to penetrate the U.S. market. There is no doubt that the share decline experienced by the "big three" automakers was predicated on the superior value provided by Toyota and other Japanese manufacturers. American car buyers had learned over a period of decades about the kind of value that Ford, for example, was providing. Quality had been declining while prices continued to rise. Customers had learned about the level of value to be expected from the American automotive industry. When Japanese cars entered the U.S. market, however, customers learned of new levels of quality at comparable or even better prices, resulting in greater value. American manufacturers quickly learned that they would have to substantially improve quality while holding the line on prices in order to compete with the Japanese on value. But, because they had so effectively taught American consumers what levels of value to expect from American suppliers, they had to also invest heavily in re-teaching about their new, intended value propositions. In fact, Ford dedicated the 1980s to trying to convince the American public that "At Ford, quality is job one." This campaign was enacted in response to a significant quality decline and subsequent value erosion of Ford's product lines.

So-called discount airlines such as Southwest blew the wings off competitors by offering equal, if not better, service at lower prices. Delta, United, Continental, and others have not figured out how to compete against the likes of Southwest and other value-driven competitors. Flyers understand that they can get as good, if not better, service, on-time arrival, cabin service, and safe baggage delivery, all at a lower price. That's value, and customers are quick to recognize it.

## WHY VALUE AND NOT SATISFACTION?

To understand why value, rather than satisfaction, is the important component in this context, it is necessary to differentiate between a strategic measure and a tactical one. In a nutshell, strategy refers to *what* and *why,* tactics refer to *how.* Strategic measures will tell you what issues to focus attention on in order to win the war, and why. Tactical measures enable you to make corrective maneuvers in order to effectively engage a specific enemy within a specific battle. Value represents the former, and satisfaction represents the latter. Both are essential for effective competition, but for different reasons.

## Linkage to Performance

Strategic measures represent leading indicators of the organization's financial or market performance. As the organization's performance on the strategic measure (value) increases, so too, at some point, does the organization's financial or market performance (market share and profitability). Conversely, if a decline in the performance on a strategic measure is experienced, there will be a lagged decline in the organization's financial or market performance. This relationship is based on a statistical linkage between the strategic measure and some desired performance measure. Strategic measures are, by their very nature and empirical relationship with desired performance outcomes, forward-looking. The strength of their relationship with performance directly impacts their predictive power. Customer value, when properly measured, provides a robust and powerful strategic measure necessary for directing the dynamics of effective competition. Because of the value–performance linkage, organizational objectives should include not only proposed changes in market share or profitability but also changes in the organization's competitive value proposition.

Tactical measures are more of a "report card" type of measure. They are typically conducted at a transactional level and reflect the organization's performance through a rear-view mirror. Transactional measures enable the organization to assess its performance with current customers and take corrective action where appropriate. They have little or no predictive power with regard to financial or market performance. Because they focus on the organization's current customers and their reactions to current transactions, they are often referred to as measures of customer satisfaction.

Satisfaction exhibits little, if any, linkage to an organization's business performance. Take, for example, the case of a large multinational corporation that zealously tracks customer satisfaction and relates it to top-line revenue growth. The most substantial linkage they have been able to achieve is reflected in an $R^2$ of .25. This means that only 25 percent of the organization's top-line revenue is explained by the metrics of customer satisfaction. *This also means that 75 percent of top-line revenue growth is explained by factors other than customer satisfaction.* Another organization links satisfaction to a customer's willingness to do future business with the company. This linkage explains only about 6 percent of a customer's willingness to do future business. *The residual 94 percent is due to other factors.*

*Customer satisfaction has a particularly poor record of predicting market performance.* Consider the case of AT&T, which found that its customer satisfaction scores were solid but its market share was declining (Gale, 1994, p. 6). Or consider the case of a large Midwestern bank that found its customer satisfaction scores were increasing but its market share was stagnant, while a cross-town rival was experiencing declining customer satisfaction scores but higher than ever earnings per share! Taken at face value,

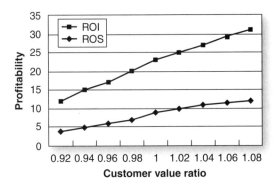

**Figure 2.2**   Customer value drives profitability.

these results would suggest that the best way to increase share and earnings is to serve your customers poorly. Of course this is nonsense, but it points out the lack of relationship that customer satisfaction has with market performance measures. It is not a good strategic measure.

The scenarios just described are, unfortunately, typical of many other organizations and their experience with customer satisfaction. Customer value, on the other hand, has a much stronger and more powerful linkage with a number of performance factors. For example, Brad Gale, author of *Managing Customer Value* (1994), notes that customer value is the best predictor of market share (p. 26). In addition, Gale has examined the relationship between customer value differentials and financial measures such as ROI and return on sales (ROS). The graph in Figure 2.2 shows the strong relationship between customer value and these two financial performance measures.

As a tactical measure, customer satisfaction at the transactional level is a beneficial and appropriate measure. It captures how satisfied a customer has been with the interaction with the organization on such factors as parts supply, billing inquiries, repairs (shop and field), technical support and so on. To the extent that these factors are related to how customers define value, satisfaction is made an even stronger tactical measure. It serves as the all-important monitoring function that allows the organization to continually assess whether it is, in fact, on track in providing the kind of customer value that differentiates it from its competitors. But for effective competitive market planning leading to increased revenue, market share, and profitability, the strategic measure of customer value is the more appropriate variable.

Value is a powerful force. We have seen it transform industries, markets, and individual firms. Organizations that learn how to manage value will be capable of deploying a very powerful strategic weapon. Creating that all-important differential value advantage leads to increased profitable share. Profitable share comes both from the acquisition of customers seeking greater value than their current suppliers can provide and from retaining customers who know that no better competitive value options are available.

# WHAT FACTORS MAKE VALUE A BETTER STRATEGIC MEASURE?

At this point in the discussion, it will be useful to delineate the specific reasons that make customer value a better strategic measure than customer satisfaction. There are three key reasons.

## Customer Value Is Market Based

First, customer value is *market based* as opposed to *customer based.* Customer satisfaction typically focuses on an organization's own customer base. Its express purpose is to identify how satisfied the organization's customers are with the organization, its products, and its services. Accordingly, most customer satisfaction models typically ignore competitors' customers. Absent input from competitors' customers, it is easy to understand why customer satisfaction cannot predict market share. It cannot account for the dynamic give and take within a competitive setting because it tends to ignore those factors that give rise to this dynamism.

Customer value, on the other hand, typically incorporates not only the organization's customers but also those of its competitors. The metrics of customer value are attentive to how well an organization addresses the factors that define value relative to how well competitors address the individual drivers of value. This is the relativity or competitiveness of value discussed earlier. Failure to understand how an organization's competitors are managing their own competitive value proposition makes competing for customers difficult at best and stupid at worse. It is akin to a general about to open battle against an enemy he or she knows nothing about. What is the strength of the enemy's troops? Their deployment? Their weaponry? Their weaknesses? A general who cannot answer the questions will certainly be at a disadvantage.

## Customer Value Equals Worth

Second, customer value addresses the "worth it" question. The most feared words a manager can hear are, "Your products or services are not worth it." And, if your products or services aren't worth what the customer pays for them, the likelihood of continued usage or repeat purchase drops precipitously.

The "worth it" question requires the ability to examine the interaction between the different quality elements and the price that the customer pays to acquire this quality bundle. Going back to the restaurant value example, the diner would evaluate the different attributes of quality of food, service, atmosphere, and whatever else was important, relative to the price that he or she paid and then ask the question, "was the experience worth it?" The metrics of customer value, if properly deployed and utilized, capture this critical interaction between quality and price.

Customer satisfaction, on the other hand, typically treats price as merely one of the many product or service attributes. This methodology treats price independently and does not look at how it interacts with the quality factors. For example, most customer satisfaction surveys ask respondents to rate either the importance and/or the organization's performance on the different quality and price attributes, and then ranks them in terms of their ratings. This typically produces a list of the importance or performance of the individual attributes and the organization's performance scores from high to low. It is very common to see that respondents have rated price as one of the most important attributes, or an attribute on which the organization is performing poorly, using this methodology. The customer satisfaction methodology, by not accounting for the interaction of price and quality, too often overemphasizes price. This overemphasis results in many organizations believing that they have a pricing problem when, in fact, what they really have is a value problem. Equally important, it fails to capture the real dynamics of the customer choice decision.

## Customer Value Is a Cognitive Measure

Third, customer satisfaction reflects an emotion. Satisfaction is akin to happiness. If you are satisfied, you are happy; if you are dissatisfied, you are unhappy. This is a state of emotional being that can be very ephemeral, changing dramatically from one transaction to another. Customer value, on the other hand, is a cognitive response, one that is based on an evaluative process. It requires the consideration and evaluation of alternatives. Most choice decisions are cognitive in nature and require the consideration of alternatives. Accordingly, customer value is based on more realistic and less simplistic assumptions.

Value is a powerful shaper of industries, markets, and competition. It is not new. What is new is our ability to effectively measure value, and with this capability comes the ability to manage it. Enterprises now have the power to manage their competitive spaces and actually shape the future of their industries. This power only exists if organizations choose to harness it. Failure to do so means that the organization is ignoring a very compelling reality governing the marketplace. Failure to do so means that the organization is competing for customers without the most important tool it can bring to bear within the competitive arena. The next two Chapters will describe more fully the tools used to effectively measure customer value and increase market share. Chapter 3 describes the tools used to acquire customers new to the market or attract customers from the competition. Chapter 4 describes tools used to enhance the loyalty of customers once you have acquired them. Both are essential for profitable increases in market share.

# 3

# Growing Market Share with Value: Customer Acquisition

Collecting market perspectives on value is a necessary first step in determining how your organization will compete for profitable increases in market share. Merely collecting and reporting survey data, however, does not make customer value an effective strategic weapon. In order for customer value to serve a strategic purpose, the data must be analyzed in such a way as to identify competitive value opportunities that the organization can leverage into greater customer acquisition and retention.

Four basic value tools serve this purpose. In order to effectively compete for customers, the organization must have four essential pieces of information: (1) the organization must know how its strategically targeted markets define value, (2) how the organization's competitive value proposition stands up within the marketplace, (3) the degree and nature of the vulnerability of the organization's competitors, and (4) the degree and nature of the loyalty of the organization's customer base. Specific tools create the actionable information that enables the organization to both acquire new customers and retain its current customers, the essence of competing for customers. The tools are: the value model, the competitive value matrix, the vulnerability matrix and the customer loyalty matrix. These tools drive the process that generates a clear and detailed roadmap for increased profitable market share. Collectively they make the competition for customers a systematic and logical process. This Chapter focuses on the first three tools for customer acquisition. The customer loyalty matrix is given special emphasis in Chapter 4.

# THE VALUE MODEL:
# THE INFORMATION PLATFORM

The value model is the strategic platform from which is launched the organization's competitive initiative for increasing market share. It is much more than a simple market research report. It is the strategic foundation that directs all subsequent activities for creating the differential value advantage.

Value models are unique to specific product lines and market segments. Market segments define value differently for different types of products, a distinction that will be addressed more fully in Chapter 5. One such model for printing equipment sold to large container manufacturers is shown in Figure 3.1. These printing machines are sold to container manufacturers for the printing of labels and other information on cardboard boxes.

The value model is empirically derived from market ratings of supplier performance on relevant attributes. It's important to note that these are not just survey responses from the customers of a single supplier, but from customers of all key suppliers of such printing machines to container manufac-

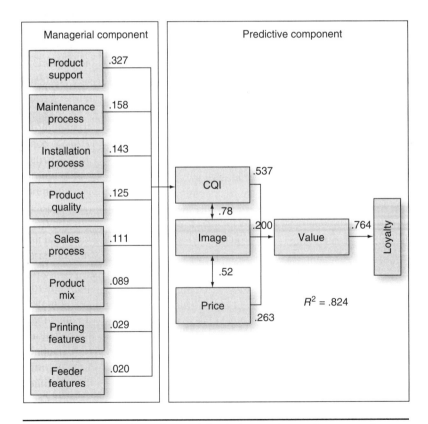

**Figure 3.1** Competitive value model: printing equipment/large container manufacturers.

turers. Effectively competing to acquire and retain customers requires an understanding of value within the dynamics of the marketplace. Limiting that understanding to one's own customers would be myopic and misleading, at best. The information that is used to generate the models comes from surveys of both the organization's customers and customers of its competitors.

The value model has two main components: a predictive component and a managerial component. The predictive component consists of the three main drivers of value: quality (CQI, or customer quality index), image, and price. The coefficients adjacent to each of these value drivers indicate how important each driver is in the value definition. In this case, the quality component (CQI) has the greatest effect (.537), followed by price (.263) and image (.200). The predictive component of the model reflects the tradeoffs among the three main value drivers and demonstrates their interaction in defining value. This interaction is critical to the understanding of value as a driver of customer loyalty and a predictor of market share. The interaction of quality, image, and price is what makes value such a powerful strategic measure. The organization that can empirically validate this interaction will be far less inclined to reflexively lower prices in order to enhance its value position. Instead, that organization will now recognize that improvements in its quality offering will have a significantly and substantially greater impact on value.

The Robustners of the model is reflected in the $R^2$ statistic of .824. $R^2$ can range between 0 and 1.00, and provides a measure of how well the independent variables (quality, image, and price) capture the meaning of the dependent variable (value). The higher the $R^2$, the more robust or better the model. This statistic also reveals to the degree of predictability that the model provides.

The managerial component of the model addresses the question "How do we improve our quality?" The individual quality drivers are identified on the far left side of the model, with the corresponding coefficients indicating their relative importance. The most important quality driver is product support (.327) followed by maintenance process (.158), and so forth.

Each of the quality drivers is empirically derived based on survey responses, and each consists of multiple performance attributes. The quality driver "product support process," for example, is comprised of seven individual performance attributes:

- Manufacturer's prompt delivery of emergency spare parts

- Availability of routine maintenance parts

- Ability to talk to the right person to help you with a complex technical problem

- Prompt manufacturer response to your technical service problems

- Prompt manufacturer response to your requests for product information

- Length of warranty period

- History of reputable service from the manufacturer

These individual attributes provide high levels of actionability for competitive planning, and also enable assessments of model reliability and validity (see technical notes in Appendix A).

It is worth noting that in this model developed for a manufacturer of printing equipment, many of the quality drivers are associated not only with the manufacturer but also with the distributor of the equipment. For example, the manufacturer and the distributor share responsibilities regarding product support, maintenance, and installation, the top three quality drivers. This is typical of many value models across a variety of industries, which is why it is important to expand the scope of thinking and competitive planning past the manufacturing process to include the entire value stream. It is axiomatic that value at the point of production does not necessarily translate into value at the point of use or consumption. Value is either added or diminished at every point along the organization's value stream. Failure to incorporate the entire value stream in competitive market planning is typically the result of a reductionistic view of value, and is guaranteed to thwart any attempts at improving the organization's competitive value proposition. The value model is the information platform that produces the other three key value tools necessary for the development of effective and actionable competitive strategies.

## THE COMPETITIVE VALUE MATRIX: THE STRATEGIC RADAR SCREEN

The competitive value matrix is the organization's radar screen. It is the tool that details the competitive landscape, laying out the competitive value propositions of each of the key players. A typical competitive value matrix is shown in Figure 3.2. The two key components of value—quality and price—are used to create the four-quadrant matrix. These two components are not only the most important drivers of value in most cases, but are also the two components most directly under the control of management. The price component constitutes market *reactions* to each supplier's pricing, not the actual price points. This distinction is important because competitive market planning includes not only the pricing of products and services, but also the organization's communications about pricing. Moreover, perceptions of quality are highly correlated with perceptions of pricing, and it is important to capture that interaction. The market means on quality and price are used to divide the matrix into the four quadrants. Image ratings are included just outside the matrix.

Competitors are positioned on the matrix based upon their scores for the two value components. Competitors residing within the upper right-hand quadrant (XYZ in this case) are those that are rated by customers as providing superior quality at a highly satisfactory price. These are the outstanding value providers. They are in a position to leverage their outstanding value proposition into increased market share. The strategic goal of these organizations is to sustain and grow their value advantage.

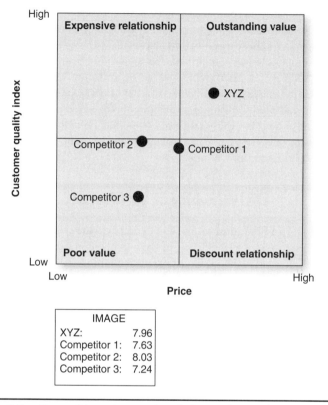

**Figure 3.2**   Competitive value matrix: printing equipment/large container manufacturers.

Those competitors located in the upper left-hand quadrant (none in this example) are those that are providing superior quality but at a less-than-satisfactory price. They provide their customers with an expensive relationship.

In the lower left-hand quadrant are the poor value competitors (Competitors 1, 2, and 3). They are providing inferior quality at a less-than satisfactory price. This position is not sustainable, and if not corrected will lead to significant share loss.

The discount relationship competitors (none in this example) are those that provide inferior quality at a price that is deemed satisfactory.

The competitive value matrix reveals the organization's existing competitive value proposition, not necessarily the one the organization thinks it has or wants to possess. It reflects in the most general terms how the market actually understands and evaluates the value the organization provides through its products and services. This is the competitive value proposition that requires active management. Failure to actively manage the organization's competitive value proposition means that its management is placed in the hands of your competition. The relative nature of value means that, as a competing supplier enhances its competitive value proposition, the competitive value proposition of your organization necessarily declines. By not actively managing your organization's competitive value proposition, you will be relinquishing control over the key factor that drives your market share.

The competitive value matrix and its underlying components also provide the roadmap for determining how an organization will compete. The matrix itself reveals the overall value position of each competitor, and each competitor's strengths and weaknesses on the key value drivers of quality and price. But both the CQI and price components of value can be further disaggregated into their constituent parts, thereby revealing very specific organizational strengths and weaknesses.

## DRIVER-LEVEL ANALYSIS

For example, profiling the various competitors on the quality drivers provides further insight into the nature of the organization's competitive value proposition. Consider the quality (CQI) drivers (Table 3.1) for Company XYZ, which sells printing equipment to large container manufacturers.

The CQI is comprised of the eight quality drivers that were identified within the value model. A head-to-head comparison indicates that Company XYZ has several significant advantages over its competition. For example, it enjoys an advantage over Competitor 3 on the CQI and all quality drivers and price. It clearly enjoy a value advantage over Competitor 3. With respect to Competitor 2, Company XYZ is also in a strong position. It has advantages on all the quality drivers with the exceptions of installation process, sales process

**Table 3.1** Driver-level analysis.

|  | XYZ | Competitor 1 | Competitor 2 | Competitior 3 |
|---|---|---|---|---|
|  | Mean | Mean | Mean | Mean |
| CQI | 7.65 | 7.56 | 7.47 | 6.88 |
| Product support | 7.63 | 7.15 | 7.40 | 6.89 |
| Maintenance process | 7.10 | 7.05 | 6.83 | 6.27 |
| Installation process | 7.52 | 7.64 | 7.41 | 6.67 |
| Product quality | 7.69 | 7.36 | 7.35 | 7.00 |
| Sales process | 7.72 | 7.67 | 7.56 | 6.72 |
| Product mix | 7.92 | 8.01 | 7.57 | 7.29 |
| Printing features | 7.26 | 7.32 | 6.21 | 6.48 |
| Feeder features | 7.03 | 7.38 | 7.60 | 6.41 |
| Price | 7.02 | 6.41 | 6.81 | 6.38 |

☐ **XYZ advantage**　　▨ **XYZ disadvantage**

and feeder features. With regard to the installation and sales processes, Company XYZ is at parity with Competitor 2, but it has a disadvantage on feeder features. With respect to Competitor 1, its closest rival, Company XYZ is at parity on all the quality drivers except for product support and product quality, where it has an advantage. Company XYZ has a disadvantage on feeder features relative to Competitor 1. As depicted on the competitive value matrix, Company XYZ has an advantage on price over all competitors.

# ATTRIBUTE-LEVEL ANALYSIS

Further information can be gleaned regarding the nature of these advantages and disadvantages by examining the individual attributes (value performance criteria, VPC) that make up the specific drivers. For example, Table 3.2 shows the different attributes that comprise the "product support" driver.

**Table 3.2**   VPC-level analysis.

|  | XYZ | Competitor 1 | Competitor 2 | Competitior 3 |
|---|---|---|---|---|
|  | Mean | Mean | Mean | Mean |
| **Product support process** | 7.65 | 7.56 | 7.47 | 6.88 |
| Manufacturer's prompt delivery ofemergency spare parts | 8.25 | 7.25 | 7.06 | 7.00 |
| Availability of routine maintenance parts | 8.33 | 7.72 | 7.68 | 7.78 |
| Ability to talk to the right person to help you with a complex technical problem | 8.11 | 7.44 | 6.99 | 6.71 |
| Prompt manufacturer response to your technical problems | 8.22 | 7.44 | 7.28 | 7.38 |
| Prompt manufacturer response to your requests for product information | 8.57 | 8.15 | 7.62 | 5.74 |
| Length of warranty period | 7.61 | 8.48 | 7.54 | 5.98 |
| History of reputable service from the manufacturer | 7.76 | 7.63 | 7.15 | 6.80 |

|  | XYZ advantage |  | XYZ disadvantage |
|---|---|---|---|

These are the actual questionnaire items that comprise the quality driver "product support process." They are the questions that all survey respondents used to evaluate the performance (1 = poor, 10 = excellent) of the several printing equipment suppliers in this market. The breakdown of this quality driver reveals that Company XYZ has strong advantages over Competitors 1, 2, and 3 on nearly all aspects of the overall product support process. With respect to Competitor 3, XYZ has advantages on all value performance criteria. The only parity situation XYZ has with regards to Competitor 2 involves the length of the warranty period. On all other value performance criteria, Company XYZ enjoys advantages. Regarding Competitor 1, XYZ's closest competitor (see Figure 3.2), XYZ has advantages on all value performance criteria that comprise this quality driver with the exception of "history of reputable service from this manufacturer," where XYZ is at parity.

This type of head-to-head comparison of competitive advantages and disadvantages provides detailed and powerful information regarding how Company XYZ can differentiate itself from its competitors, especially Competitor 1, and improve its competitive value proposition. This is the subject of Chapter 7.

The competition for new customers is focused on two sources, those new to the market and those currently buying from other suppliers. In either case, the organization's competitive value proposition, as indicated in the competitive value matrix, will be a deciding factor in who wins the competition for these new customers. The organization's existing value proposition is what new entrants to the market use to evaluate both the quality of the organization's offering and the price that they will have to pay to get it. It tells them which organization offers the best deal and which organization's product and/or service offerings just aren't worth it. The dissemination of this information may take some time as buyers try different offerings. What can be expected is that the market will communicate this value message to all customers. This value-shopping process is clearly discernible in the ongoing competition among Internet service providers (ISP)s, wireless telecom suppliers, and cable companies, among others.

Prying customers away from their current suppliers is a more costly proposition. Habit and relationships make many customers less willing to shop around. However, there typically comes a time when a buyer is under pressure, from either a cost or performance standpoint, and initiates a search for an alternative supplier. When this occurs, value—the relationship between the quality of an organization's product/service offering and its cost—becomes critical in the choice decision. Here, again, the organization's competitive value proposition is a key criterion in the evaluation process.

# THE VULNERABILITY MATRIX: A POWERFUL ACQUISITION TOOL

The competition for customers is focused on two fronts: the acquisition of new customers and the retention of current customers. Coupled with the competitive value matrix, the vulnerability matrix provides a powerful tool for identifying competitors "low-hanging fruit," those customers who do not feel that they are receiving the kind of value they deserve. As such, it is an important tool for the acquisition of new customers. A typical vulnerability matrix is shown in Figure 3.3.

The vulnerability matrix is set up in the same way as the competitive value matrix, with the CQI on the vertical axis and price on the horizontal axis. The same four quadrants are formed by dissecting each axis at the market mean. The difference is that instead of locating competitors on the map, the circles represent groups of customers of a specific competitor. The vulnerability matrix is a powerful competitive intelligence tool for identifying the extent of a competitor's weaknesses. Because the midpoints of the two axes are based on *market* means, all the groups of a competitor's customers could be located in the upper-right quadrant. If this were the case, that competitor would be exhibiting a very low degree of vulnerability—all its

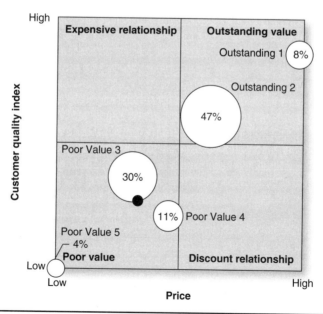

**Figure 3.3** Competitive vulnerability matrix—Competitor 1.

customers would be reporting that they are receiving better than average value from their current supplier. To the extent that groups of a competitor's customers are dispersed around the market means, as is the case in Figure 3.3, the competitor has specific vulnerabilities. As before, the CQI, price, and image components can be broken down to reveal the precise nature of those vulnerabilities, which will be somewhat different for each group of customers.

For example, Competitor 1, Company XYZ's closest rival, has two groups of customers that indicate they are receiving outstanding value—high quality at a highly satisfying price. These are the most loyal customers of Competitor 1, the least likely to defect and, hence, the most difficult to target for acquisition. Together they account for about 55 percent of Competitor 1's collective customer base. The other 45 percent is quite a different matter.

There are three groups of customers (Groups 3, 4, and 5), indicating that they are receiving poor value from Competitor 1. These are active shoppers; they seek to defect when another and better value opportunity comes along. The utility of the vulnerability matrix resides in its ability to identify who these vulnerable customers are and why they are vulnerable. This can be done on several levels.

The value groups can be profiled in terms of their scores on each of the quality drivers and their constituent value performance criteria. Knowing the reasons why Competitor 1's customers are not receiving outstanding value provides important information for driving specific advertising and promotional programs. For example, with the information from Competitor 1's vulnerability matrix, Company XYZ's salespeople now know that every time they are calling on a customer of Competitor 1, there is a 45 percent probability that they are calling on a customer who is not getting the requisite level of value from the chosen supplier. Each of those three groups of Competitor 1's customers is reporting lower-than-average satisfaction with Competitor 1's prices. But, from a strategic standpoint, it's at least as important to understand the basis for their perceptions of poor quality because if these also happen to be areas of strength for XYZ, Competitor 1's "low-hanging fruit" can be picked without negotiating on the basis of price. The basis for customer perceptions of poor quality is revealed in Table 3.3.

Clearly, Groups 3, 4, and 5 are reporting lower levels of quality (CQI) from Competitor 1 than are Groups 1 and 2. But the bases for those perceptions of poor quality differ from group to group. Competitor 1 is most vulnerable with Group 3 (30 percent of the competitor's customer base) on the basis of the installation process, product quality, and the sales process. Group 5 (4 percent of Competitor 1's customer base) also reports low levels of quality in the product and the sales process, but this group is also displeased with the maintenance process, the product mix, and printing features. Competitor 1's key vulnerabilities with Group 4 (11 percent) lie in the areas of its product support process, the maintenance process, and printing features.

These customer groups can then be profiled on the basis of any firm-specific information collected during the survey to further pinpoint the types

**Table 3.3**   Quality driver analysis—Competitor 1.

| | Group 1 | Group 2 | Group 3 | Group 4 | Group 5 |
|---|---|---|---|---|---|
| CQI | 9.93 | 8.12 | 5.81 | 5.45 | 3.85 |
| Product support process | 9.97 | 8.23 | 6.57 | 4.69 | 7.11 |
| Maintenance process | 9.93 | 7.52 | 6.6 | 3.95 | 2.5 |
| Installation process | 9.98 | 8.17 | 5.42 | 5.81 | 8.02 |
| Product quality | 9.82 | 8.29 | 4.27 | 5.62 | 2.58 |
| Sales process | 9.9 | 8.45 | 4.63 | 6.21 | 2.71 |
| Produt mix | 9.98 | 8.28 | 6.31 | 7.32 | 1.12 |
| Printing features | 9.8 | 6.43 | 6.12 | 3.76 | 3.33 |
| Feeder features | 9.93 | 8.19 | 6.56 | 6.04 | 4.98 |
| Price | 9.68 | 7.16 | 5.7 | 6.43 | 2.75 |

Table 3.3 shows the mean performance scores on a scale of 1–10 where 1 = poor performance and 10 = superior performance.

of customers most likely to be resident in each of these poor value groups. In addition, depending on what information has been collected, the value, in economic terms (sales; number of orders; dollars spent on parts, service, and other downstream revenues), of each customer can be calculated to provide a basis for assessing the potential return on acquisition efforts. This keeps the focus on the acquisition of profitable customers and profitable market share. This is precisely the type of information that brings life to competitive planning initiatives, driving objectives and action programs directly into operational and sales processes.

These are the value tools that will enable your organization to acquire new customers, whether by attracting customers new to the market with a superior value proposition or by capitalizing on the value vulnerabilities of key competitors. The next Chapter will describe the tools used to retain and enhance the loyalty of those customers once they are doing business with your organization.

# 4

# Growing Market Share with Value: Customer Retention

From the perspective of an organization's sales team, there is nothing quite so glamorous or exciting as the acquisition of new customers. And this perspective is often reinforced within the organization through the types of sales incentives provided and the overall philosophy of senior management about how to grow market share. But, aside from the fact that this is only half the formula for increasing market share, it's also the more expensive half. Often forgotten in the competition for customers and market share is the importance of the organization's current customer base. These are the customers whose retention lies at the heart of *profitable* increases in market share.

Your current customer base consists of those who would never consider buying another brand from another supplier, as well as those who purchase and use your products on a periodic basis. The grocery shopper who shops your store one out of every three shopping trips is a current customer, just as is the Ford customer who would never consider buying a brand other than Ford. Part of the challenge regarding the retention of current customers, of course, lies in determining which of those are actually profitable customers and which would contribute more to your bottom line by becoming someone else's customer.

Putting that issue aside for the moment (we'll return to it later in the Chapter), much of the emphasis on market share increases in many companies comes from an undue focus on the acquisition of new customers, frequently at the expense of customer retention. This practice is becoming more and more expensive, often leading to unwise attempts to reduce other costs that are actually necessary in providing outstanding value to current customers. In fact, many industry experts correctly note that the cost of customer acquisition, depending on the industry, can run 5 to 10 times the cost of customer retention.

One business-to-business (B2B) telecommunications firm illustrates the point. This organization, not unlike many of its competitors, had a single-minded focus on the acquisition of new customers. Sales compensation was based on the generation of new revenue. No one in the organization was rewarded for retaining current customers, much less for enhancing the loyalty of those customers. Billing systems were broken and problem resolution was abysmal. Even the delivery of new equipment was typically delayed because sales personnel were too busy chasing new business to correctly complete the necessary paperwork. This organization was losing about half its customers every year. But the unofficial strategy of the organization was simply to "out-sell churn." In other words, if 50 percent of customers were defecting, sales members were compelled to generate at least 51 percent new customers if they were to be compensated. Like the Queen in *Alice through the Looking Glass,* they were destined to run harder and harder simply to stay in place.

Although this may be an extreme example, the underlying philosophy is not that uncommon. This organization is not alone in its deliberate focus on customer acquisition. A recent study reported on emarketer.com (June 14, 2005) revealed that customer acquisition was cited as the number-one goal of B2B marketers in 2004, slipping slightly to second in 2005. Customer retention was the goal least cited by B2B marketers for both years.

Customer loss is inevitable. In fact, in an oft-repeated study of customer defections ("The Value of Customer Retention,", 2005), the following reasons for defection are reported:

- Move or die                            4 percent

- Other company friendship               5 percent

- Competition                            9 percent

- Product dissatisfaction                15 percent

- **No customer contact strategy**       **67 percent**

The lack of a customer contact strategy strongly suggests that companies are taking their current customers for granted and that most of their market share efforts are focused on adding new customers to their base. That this is a mistake is probably all too obvious, even to the most casual reader. But it begs the question, *Why would any organization take for granted the very customers that would provide an annuity?* And the answers to that question typically lie in the organization's failure to understand the drivers of quality and value in their targeted markets, their failure to understand where and how the organization is failing in delivering on those drivers, and their failure to understand the cost implications of those failures. Any strategy to compete effectively for customers simply cannot ignore the role of value in retaining currently profitable customers.

# THE VALUE OF CUSTOMER LOYALTY

Although the importance of developing loyal customers may seem intuitively obvious, there is no need to rely upon intuition alone. There is ample evidence of both the direct and indirect economic impact of loyal customers. First, we will look at the direct economic impact.

Study after study and analysis after analysis point out that loyal customers are the most profitable customers. One such study by Walker International (Walker Loyalty Report for Communications Services, 2005) typifies the findings. According to Walker Information Executive Vice President Phil Bounsall:

> Customer loyalty absolutely correlates to hard, tangible business outcomes. Companies that have more loyal customers seem to have competitive advantages that impact financial results and other key performance metrics, including shareholder value.

The author goes on to point out:

> Across the industry, Loyalty Leaders significantly outperform Loyalty Laggards. The annual average revenue growth rate of Loyalty Leaders over a three year period exceeds the comparable rate of Loyalty Laggards by 20 percentage points and the three-year average operating margin of Loyalty Leaders is 22 percentage points higher than the comparable results for Loyalty Laggards. The percentage change in stock price over five years is 34 points higher for Loyalty Leaders as compared to Loyalty Laggards.

In a 2003 article, "Winning Customer Loyalty Is the Key to a Winning CRM Strategy," Rigby, Reichheld, and Dawson point to a Bain & Company study citing the financial results from customer loyalty:

> A five percent increase in customer retention increases profits by 25–95 percent. The reason? It costs so much more to acquire customers that many of these relationships are unprofitable in the early years. Only later, when the cost of serving loyal customers falls and the volume of their purchases rises, do relationships generate big returns.

Other reasons for this loyalty profitability link are offered by Buchanan and Gilles (1990):

- Account maintenance costs decline as a percentage of total costs (or as a percentage of revenue).

- Long-term customers tend to be less inclined to switch, and also tend to be less price sensitive. This can result in stable unit sales volume and increases in dollar-sales volume.

- Long-term customers are more likely to purchase ancillary products and high-margin supplemental products.

- Customers that stay with you tend to be satisfied with the relationship and are less likely to switch to competitors, making market entry or competitors' market share gain more difficult.

- Regular customers tend to be less expensive to service because they are familiar with the process, require less "education," and are consistent in their order placement.

Finally, loyal customers are more recession proof, according to McConnell and Huba (2002, p. 4):

> The recession of 2000–2002 was no different. Two million people were laid off in the United States. A record of 257 publicly traded companies filed for bankruptcy in 2001, representing a 46 percent increase over the prior year's record of 176 filings.

> Yet some businesses rode out the recession without layoffs (or with only minimal furloughs), steady profitability, and minimal budget cuts, if any. These standout companies were successful despite economic turmoil. In researching this phenomenon, we discovered similarities in the customer base of seven separate companies: Each had spent previous years maniacally focusing on delighting customers and building loyal, passionate fans who would continue to support the business through times of economic distress.

These are but a few of the more recent findings pertaining to the direct economic impact of customer loyalty. But what of the less direct impacts of developing loyal customers? Consider the attributes of a customer evangelist (a very loyal customer), as defined by McConnell and Huba (2002):

- They purchase and believe in your product or service

- They are loyal and passionately recommend you to friends, neighbors and colleagues

- They purchase your products as gifts for others

- They provide unsolicited feedback or praise

- They forgive occasional dips in service and quality but let you know when quality slips

- They are not bought; customer evangelists extol your virtues freely

This last point is particularly relevant to organizations that try to create "sticky customers" through so-called loyalty programs. Certainly many business travelers, and probably many leisure travelers as well, participate in airline and hotel loyalty programs. These programs may cause the individual consumer to "stick with" a certain airline in order to maximize free travel miles and upgrades, or to "stick with" a certain hotel chain for free room nights, but this is frequently a grudging "stickiness." When those consumers talk with others about their experiences with airlines and hotels, they rarely discuss those experiences in terms of the loyalty programs. Rather, they talk about those key quality drivers most important to them, relative to the price they had to pay to receive those benefits. In other words, evangelists are created by providing superior value, not by buying loyalty with member rewards.

McConnell and Huba (2002) go on to cite a study released in 2001 by Euro RSCG Worldwide identifying how customers get their information regarding technology products, which emphasizes this very point:

- 13 percent from advertising
- 20 percent from Web sites
- **34 percent from word of mouth**

The source of the "excitement factor" about a tech product or service was equally revealing:

- 0 percent from radio
- 1 percent from billboards
- 4 percent from TV ads
- 4 percent from print ads
- 15 percent from magazines
- **40 percent from referrals by colleagues or family**

Loyal customers are your organization's best salespeople! The challenge facing every business organization is to identify their most loyal customers and, by extension, those who are less loyal, identifying the causative factors driving that loyalty, and enhancing the loyalty of those customers who are most economically valuable to the organization.

## ASSESSING CUSTOMER LOYALTY

So, how loyal is your customer base? Effectively competing for customers requires this knowledge because it's only through enhancing the loyalty of your most profitable customers that you will have the resources necessary to acquire additional new customers. If you don't know how loyal your customer base is or how profitable it is, your ability to compete is severely limited.

We've alluded to the fact that customer loyalty, and certainly customer evangelism, cannot be bought but must be earned through the delivery of superior value. So it makes sense to assess the loyalty of your current customer base in terms of the value they are getting from you. This means that that assessment must be based on those very drivers of value described in the

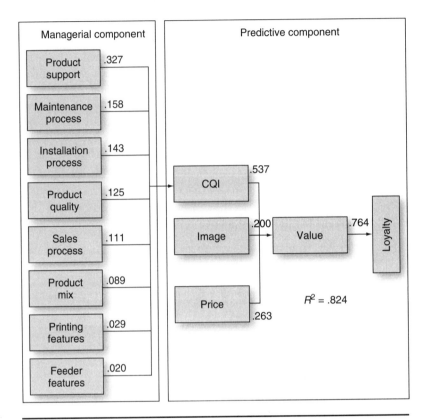

**Figure 4.1**   Customer value model: printing equipment/large container manufacturers.

previous Chapter. Let's revisit the value model for printing equipment sold to large container manufacturers (Figure 4.1), first described in Chapter 3.

This value model serves as the platform for development of the customer loyalty matrix. Once again, the key drivers of value—quality (CQI) and price—are used to plot the loyalty of Company XYZ's current customer base. Image ratings are reported alongside the matrix. As is the case with the vulnerability matrix, the means of each of these value drivers divide the vertical and horizontal axes to produce the 2 × 2 matrix. The use of market means is important because customers must be acquired (vulnerability matrix) and retained (customer loyalty matrix, Figure 4.2) against the dynamics of market competition.

Moreover, the use of market means implies that all groups of XYZ's customers could be located in the "outstanding value" quadrant, though that may not be the most desirable or profitable position to be in.

Value is the most managerially useful predictor of customer loyalty. The greater the value customers experience, the greater the loyalty they

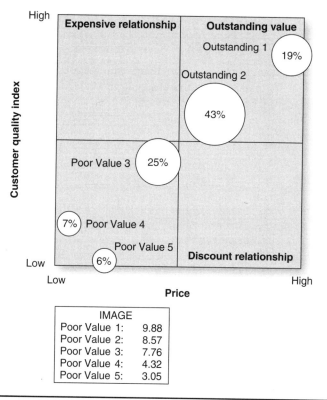

**Figure 4.2**  The customer loyalty matrix.

manifest. Frederich Reichheld (2003) has developed a compelling argument, supported by considerable empirical evidence, that a customer's willingness to recommend a company's product or service to a friend is the best single indicator of that customer's loyalty. He notes that the customer's willingness to recommend a product or service is a stronger indicator of customer loyalty than even repeat purchase behavior, because customers who make repeat purchases may be trapped by inertia, indifference, or exit barriers created by the company. And value is an incredibly strong predictor of "willingness to recommend," as shown in Table 4.1.

In fact, on this basis, value typically accounts for 75 to 85 percent of the customer's willingness to recommend the organization's products and services. Moreover, as shown in Table 4.1, value translates into specific behaviors that are advantageous to the organization, such as an *unwillingness* to switch to another supplier, even at substantial price discounts. Value is the velcro that attaches a customer to an organization, creating that all important loyalty that makes each customer a potential salesperson.

**Table 4.1**    Recommendation and switching intentions by value groups.

| | Value Groups | | | | |
|---|---|---|---|---|---|
| | Outstanding 1 | Outstanding 2 | Poor Value 3 | Poor Value 4 | Poor Value 5 |
| | Mean | Mean | Mean | Mean | Mean |
| **Q6.** How likely are you to recommend **XYZ?*** | 4.90 | 4.59 | 4.19 | 1.60 | 2.00 |
| **Q7.** How likely are you to switch at a 10% price savings?** | 3.5 | 3.1 | 2.45 | 1.37 | 1.00 |

*1 = very unlikely, 5 = likely
**1 = very likely, 5 = unlikely

   The point is that although the customer's "willingness to recommend" is a very strong indicator of customer loyalty, by itself, it serves no useful managerial function. In order to effectively compete for customers, and to enhance the loyalty of your current customer base, you need to understand the interactions among quality, image, and price as reflected in the value models, and you need to understand the relevance of key quality drivers for any interventions designed to enhance customer loyalty.

# USING THE CUSTOMER LOYALTY MATRIX FOR INTERVENTIONS

The customer loyalty matrix can be used for two specific types of interventions: individual interventions and systemic interventions. Individual interventions are best driven by individual transactions experienced by customers, and will be addressed further in Chapter 10. This value tool is made even more powerful when it is linked to the organization's customer relationship management (CRM) system.

   Because the "bubbles" in the customer loyalty matrix are comprised of the organization's own customers, there is individual information on each of the customers. Customers in any value group can be linked to purchase history; frequency of purchase; amount spent on products, service, and parts; service calls; frequency of times the customer has called for a problem, and so on. It is limited only by the quality and the quantity of information within the organization's CRM system. This information is important because the management of any individual within, say, a poor value group will be dependent upon the economic value of the individual to the organization. Statistics such as lifetime value of the customer (LVC) can be calculated as an indicator of

**Table 4.2**   Quality and driver scores by value groups.

| | Outstanding Value 1 | Outstanding Value 2 | Poor Value 3 | Poor Value 4 | Poor Value 5 |
|---|---|---|---|---|---|
| Product support process | 8.23 | 7.75 | 6.51 | 5.02 | 3.48 |
| Maintenance process | 7.9 | 7.85 | 5.97 | 5.1 | 4.11 |
| Installation process | 7.98 | 7.64 | 5.87 | 5.09 | 4.23 |
| Product quality | 7.69 | 7.38 | 6 | 4.97 | 3.98 |
| Sales process | 7.72 | 7.67 | 6.23 | 4.83 | 4.12 |
| Product mix | 7.92 | 8.01 | 6.51 | 5.13 | 4.25 |
| Printing features | 7.26 | 7.32 | 6.21 | 5.48 | 4.86 |
| Feeder features | 7.03 | 7.38 | 6.56 | 5.41 | 4.59 |
| Price | 8.56 | 7.43 | 5.45 | 3.58 | 4.58 |

this economic value. Those customers with high economic value should receive greater attention, both in terms of the quality of the response and the speed of the response, than those customers with much less value to the firm.

Knowing the overall loyalty distribution of an organization's customer base is interesting but not very managerially useful, unless the loyalty matrix can also provide information about the types of interventions required to enhance the loyalty of economically valuable customers. To that end, individual quality driver scores can be calculated for each customer group such as those shown in Table 4.2.

Table 4.2 reveals the basis of poor value for those customers in the three different poor value groups. This information can provide useful direction for improving the organization's value offering. Poor Value Group 3, for example, rates Company XYZ lowest on the maintenance process and the installation process, while Poor Value Group 4 rates XYZ lowest on product quality and the sales process. Further investigation of weaknesses at the attribute level can provide explicit direction for process improvements.

A further analysis of Group 4's low rating for XYZ's sales performance, for example, is shown in Table 4.3.

The effectiveness of local sales reps in getting the manufacturer to respond to problems is clearly a problem for this group of customers. Moreover, this is a problem that is either people or process related. If a profile of customers within this group reveals that they are largely from one sales territory, the problem may be a personnel problem. If, however, the customers in this group are widely distributed geographically, the underlying issue is likely a process problem.

Failure analyses can also be conducted by bringing together a number of customers from each of these value groups to further explore the bases for

**Table 4.3**   Sales process Value Performance Criteria (VPC) ratings for Value
Group 4.

| Sales Process Driver | Group 4 |
|---|---|
| Local sales reps follow up on open quotes | 5.79 |
| Local sales reps follow up after equipment delivery | 4.57 |
| Effectiveness of the sales rep in getting the manufacturer to solve problems | 2.27 |
| Ability of the local sales rep to provide sound technical advice | 5.04 |
| Local sales rep not overpromising on machine performance | 5.43 |
| Technical knowledge of the manufacturer's sales personnel | 5.65 |
| Ease of contact with the local sales rep | 5.57 |
| Prompt response to a request for quotation | 4.32 |

these low ratings. By understanding how and why the organization is failing to deliver outstanding value, problems can be identified and addressed.

Poor Value Group 5 rates XYZ poorly on product quality and product support, but before taking aggressive corrective action, XYZ would do well to assess the economic value of this customer group. Experience dictates that every organization has some customers who are chronic complainers, and these customers frequently are not very profitable. The point is, specific customers can be profiled and targeted with the appropriate levels of intervention.

This leads us to the next category of interventions: systemic interventions. Instead of focusing on specific individuals, systemic interventions concentrate on failures within the system. These might be attributable to salespeople, processes, products, and distribution policies and practices.

Consider the case of the printing manufacturer used in this Chapter's discussion. Probing the poor value customers revealed some very interesting information regarding a number of factors that affected them. Their complaints focused on issues of installation, product support and maintenance, and shared responsibilities between the manufacturer and the distributor. Plotting the poor and outstanding value customers on a map overlaid by distributor sales territories reveals the situation shown in Figure 4.3.

By plotting the customers from the different value groups on the map, it becomes clear that poor value is not a random factor but rather a systematic factor attributable to specific distributors. Distributors in territories 1 and 2 are consistently associated with the delivery of poor value. Poor value customers also show up in territories 10 and 6, but not with the consistency of territories 1 and 2. Clearly, there is a distributor-related issue in territories 1 and 2. Instead of having to review policies and practices of all distributors, the organization can focus directly on those in territories 1 and 2. The re-

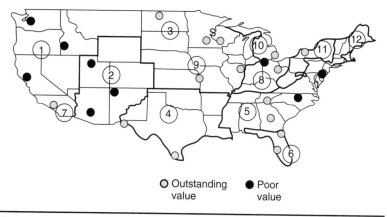

**Figure 4.3**   Poor value groups by distributor territories.

view may call for a modification of individual distributor practices but it may also call for reviewing the processes that are shared between the manufacturer and the distributor. Six Sigma projects might be directed to "fixing" these processes. In this way, the voice of the customer is directing Six Sigma initiatives that will ultimately enhance the organization's competitive value proposition, not only among its won customers but also for the market as a whole.

The customer loyalty matrix is useful for a number of reasons. Again, by profiling the various customer value groups the economic value of each group of customers can be ascertained. This economic value can be denominated in sales, margins, operating profits, or any other indicator. Each customer in each group can be linked back to the organization's internal information systems and profiled on any basis that the internal information system has available. This might include, but certainly is not limited to the following:

- Which warehouses serve which customers?

- Which salespeople are serving which customers?

- What is the purchase history of any customer?

- How many complaints are filed by a specific customer?

- What value scores are associated with each customer?

- What are the CQI and price satisfaction scores associated with each customer?

- What are the individual scores on the various attributes for specific customers?

This makes the customer loyalty matrix a particularly valuable and potent addendum to the organization's CRM system.

Taken collectively, the four value tools discussed in Chapters 3 and 4 provide a systematic and logical process by which an organization can effectively compete for customers. These tools enable the organization to identify what drives value for customers buying a specific product line, how customers define an organization's competitive value proposition relative to the organization's competitors, how vulnerable competitors' customers are to competitive intrusion and on what basis, and finally, how loyal the organization's customer base is. This information is critical in the development of actionable and effective strategies for improving the organization's competitive performance.

# Part II:
# The Competitive
# Planning Process

## Chapter 5
Choosing Where to Compete

## Chapter 6
What Is the Organization's Current Value Proposition?

## Chapter 7
What Does the Organization Want Its Competitive Value
Proposition to Be?

## Chapter 8
How Does the Organization Manage Its Value Proposition?

## Chapter 9
The Value-Strategy-Process Linkage

## Chapter 10
Monitoring Plan Effectiveness

# 5

# Choosing Where
# to Compete

The battlefield(s) on which an organization competes must be a matter of choice. Unfortunately, too often companies let their competitors choose where they will compete. Some battlefields are better suited for substantial gains than are others, and these areas are where the organization's competitive resources should be focused. Many organizations understand this conceptually, but completely ignore it in actual practice. They continue to resource unprofitable opportunities or actively invest in segments with product/services and supporting marketing efforts that have little opportunity for profitable market share growth. This is probably a residual effect of the sales orientation that dominated corporate America in the 1950s, in which any opportunity to sell was viewed as a good opportunity. But one of the lessons of the last decade was that "you can't be everything to everybody." Those organizations that continue trying to do so will find themselves on the ash heap of the business landscape, burned by those enterprises with the discipline to focus their competitive efforts. Yet, while many organizations talk about market segments and target markets, few understand how to actually put targeting of markets into practice.

Choosing where to compete is a decision that is made at the business-unit level, as shown in Figure 5.1 and discussed in detail in Chapter 1. Some organizations have multiple business units while others may have only one. Each business unit will have a number of different opportunities for competing, some of which will be better than others. This is where choice comes into play. It is not a corporate-level decision.

This Chapter addresses the question of "Where should an organization compete?" It is, perhaps, the most important question in competing for customers because it identifies the competitive arena, the competitors in that arena, and the rules of competitive engagement. In the absence of a clear decision about where to compete, there can be no effective answer to the question about how to compete.

**Figure 5.1**  Planning levels and purposes.

# FOCUS, FOCUS, FOCUS

Choosing where to compete involves achieving the proper focus. And the appropriate focus is directed by the two factors that drive company revenues: the products or services you provide and the customers who buy them. Aligning these two revenue components in a product/market matrix, shown generically in Figure 5.2, creates a decision framework for choosing where to compete.

## Product Lines

The business unit or organization's product lines are arrayed along the vertical axis. Some organizations will have many product lines; others may have only one. The key to the correct identification of product lines is to do so from the customer's perspective, not from an internal perspective. It's tempting to rely upon product definitions from an engineering perspective, because the engineering group typically designs the products and often exhibits a degree of ownership in that regard. It's equally tempting to rely upon the perspective of the accounting group, because they frequently categorize products for reporting purposes.

One example of such misidentification comes from a major equipment manufacturer in regard to its initial foray into smaller earthmoving equipment. Such equipment included products like backhoe loaders, small wheel loaders, and so forth. Because most of that equipment was driven by engines of less than 100 horsepower, someone in the engineering group decided that all this equipment would appropriately be categorized as the "Century Line." Unfortunately, no customers were seeking to acquire a "Century

| Market / Product | Market A | Market B | Market C | Market D | | | Total |
|---|---|---|---|---|---|---|---|
| Product A | | | | | | | |
| Product B | | | | | | | |
| Product C | | | | | | | |
| | | | | | | | |
| Total | | | | | | | |

**Figure 5.2** Product/market matrix.

Line." Customers were looking for backhoe loaders or wheel loaders. Marketing dollars invested in the Century Line inevitably missed the mark.

There is one simple rule that will help your organization correctly identify its product (or service) lines. Products within a product line are substitutable for one another, whereas products from different product lines are not. And, of course, the final check is how customers characterize product lines.

Products within the same product line may come in different sizes, weights, or colors, and though some sizes, weights, or colors may be more preferable to others for certain applications, they can be substituted for one another. For example, tractors may come in different horsepower sizes, and some horsepower sizes may be more suitable for particular jobs than others. That said, a small tractor can do the job of a larger tractor, albeit perhaps not as efficiently. However, a tractor cannot be used to put ore into a truck or haul goods from one coast to another. Similarly, cheeses may come in different flavors and a cook may choose between using a Swiss cheese or a cheddar cheese, but would not use a piece of pork as a substitute. While these examples may seem overly simplistic, they illustrate a key characteristic of product lines that is often ignored, leading to confusion within an organization and a lack of focus. And if there is confusion within the organization about product lines, it will undoubtedly lead to confusion within the marketplace. We have often been involved in planning sessions regarding a specific product line only to have different members of the planning team asking for clarification about the different products actually being dealt with. Without clearly defined product lines, planning becomes hazy and unfocused and the resultant competition for customers will be equally hazy and unfocused. However, focusing solely on a product line does not provide sufficient clarity for competitive planning.

## Market Segments

The other axis of the product/market matrix is comprised of markets and market segments. As you probably know, markets are groups of customers with similar needs that respond to a specific marketing mix. Customers within a market are relatively homogenous with respect to their needs and wants. That is, their needs are more similar than different from one another. Customers in different market segments tend to have somewhat different needs, or differing priorities relative to those needs. Large industrial customers of an electric utility, for example, tend to place a much greater emphasis on the price of electricity than do smaller commercial enterprises. Smaller commercial companies are more reliant on their local utility to provide energy-saving advice and to be responsive in addressing their electrical problems. A family man buying a car will likely have a very different set of needs and interests than an 18-year-old.

Markets may be further broken down into segments. This further breakdown provides yet another level of focus, enabling even more actionable plans and strategies. The degree of segmentation will often be a function of a market's size, which in turn may be a function of the organization's reach. It may be very useful for a national manufacturer of forklifts to segment its manufacturing market into applications: (1) food and beverage, (2) metals and machines, (3) building materials, and so forth. But a forklift dealer competing in a local territory might find planning at that level to be unnecessary because not all segments are represented within the local market.

Much has been written about market segmentation, and much has been spent on identifying the "perfect" segmentation scheme. One result of some of the more "sophisticated" statistical approaches to segmentation is the identification of segments that are intuitively appealing, but are not "findable." Segments such as "Service R Us" may be describable as customers who are highly dependent upon external service solutions, but if you can't identify which customers belong to the segment, the schema is managerially useless. The best test of a good segmentation approach is to place yourself in the following scenario: If a customer were to walk into your office or store, and after asking that customer a couple of basic questions, could you correctly put the customer into the proper segment? If not, more than likely your segmentation approach is flawed. One organization, having spent hundreds of thousands of dollars on an elaborate segmentation schema, found that it could only classify about 20 percent of its *own* customers accurately, and had no basis whatsoever for classifying customers of the competition.

Many organizations confuse product lines with market segments and refer to markets as the locomotive or sports car segment. Neither locomotives nor sports cars buy anything. Customers buy locomotives and sports cars. Segments must reflect the nature of the customer rather than the product. Organizations that are new to segmentation will find that segmentation is a trial-and-error exercise. There is no single set of standards for best segmentation practices—the best segmentation approach is the one that works.

## Identifying Where to Compete

Identifying where to compete will be a function of the business unit's growth objectives. The primary objective of one business unit may be to maximize market share, whereas another business unit may be challenged to maximize profits. Yet another business unit may be focused on revenue growth or increased utilization of existing facilities. Regardless of the objective, or combination of objectives, the opportunities represented by the intersections of product lines and markets are not equal. Some will be much better than others, and the challenge for the business-unit manager is to select a limited number of opportunities for selective investment of limited resources.

Each intersection of a product line and a market (segment) within a product/market matrix represents an opportunity. These intersections are called product/markets. The issue now is how to identify which opportunities are the best and merit resource investment. This is addressed by identifying specific strategic criteria by which the various opportunities can be evaluated and graded.

Strategic criteria might include, but are not necessarily limited to, the following:

- Current market share within a product/market

- Current size of a product/market

- Profitability (margins) of a product/market

- Growth rate of a product/market

- Future downstream product support (parts/repair) revenue within a product/market

- Competitive intensity within a product/market

- Lost sales within a product/market

- Synergies with other product/markets

Once the most relevant criteria are selected, they must be applied uniformly across the entire product/market matrix. Initially, this may prove to be difficult. Most organizational accounting systems are not organized to provide the kind of information a product/market matrix requires for analysis. Initial assessments therefore may not be perfect. However, eventually it is essential to align the accounting and other relevant information systems with the product/market matrix and not let your competitive efforts be stymied by the limited information that you do have. Selecting evaluative criteria on their merits relative to business-unit objectives will lead the organization to bring its accounting systems into alignment with strategic priorities.

Each viable cell within a product/market matrix should be evaluated on the basis of the selected criteria and graded as to its efficacy. This evaluation produces a prioritization of opportunities from those that are the best opportunities to those that represent the least opportunity. Some product/markets may be so minimally viable that they can be eliminated from consideration at the outset. For example, the intersection of mortgage services for the retiree market would typically represent a minimal opportunity, as would a minivan for a single person. Rather than clutter the matrix with trivial information, this product/market and others like it might be crossed out.

A simple example will illustrate the prioritization process. The product/market matrix shown in Figure 5.3 was created by a relatively small company selling equipment to manufacturers of plastics products. In this case, the company itself was a single business unit that manufactured and sold three product lines.

| Product/Market | | Low-tech | | High-tech | | Total | |
|---|---|---|---|---|---|---|---|
| Dryers | Hot air | $ .9 MIL | MODERATE | $ 1.1 MIL | MODERATE | $ 2.0 MIL | MODERATE |
| | | | MODERATE | | MOD-HIGH | -47% | MOD-HIGH |
| | | | MODERATE | | MODERATE | 11.40% | MODERATE |
| | | | | | | $ .15 MIL | $ .23 MIL |
| | Dehumidifier | $ 18. MIL | HIGH | $ 22. MIL | HIGH | $ 40. MIL | HIGH |
| | | | HIGH | | HIGH | -47% | HIGH |
| | | | MODERATE | | MODERATE | 11.40% | MODERATE |
| | | | | | | $ 2.85 MIL | $ 4.6 MIL |
| Conveying | Pressure | $1.6MIL | MOD-HIGH | $ 3.4 MIL | MOD-HIGH | $ 5. MIL | MOD-HIGH |
| | | | MOD-HIGH | | MOD-HIGH | -37% | MOD-HIGH |
| | | | MODERATE | | MODERATE | 7.20% | MODERATE |
| | | | | | | $ .08 MIL | $ .36 MIL |
| | Vacuum | $14.4MIL | HIGH | $30.6 MIL | HIGH | $ 45. MIL | HIGH |
| | | | HIGH | | HIGH | -37% | HIGH |
| | | | MODERATE | | MODERATE | 7.20% | MODERATE |
| | | | | | | $ .74 MIL | $ 3.24 MIL |
| Blenders | Gravimetric | $ 6.2 MIL | HIGH | $ 24.8 MIL | HIGH | $ 31. MIL | HIGH |
| | | | MOD-HIGH | | HIGH | -18% | MOD-HIGH |
| | | | MODERATE | | MODERATE | 1.50% | MOD |
| | | | | | | $ .16 MIL | $ .47 MIL |
| | Volumetric | $ 4.8 MIL | HIGH | $ 1.2 MIL | MODERATE | $ 6. MIL | MOD-HIGH |
| | | | MODERATE | | MODERATE | -18% | MODERATE |
| | | | MODERATE | | MODERATE | 1.50% | MODERATE |
| | | | | | | $ .04 MIL | $ .1 MIL |
| Total | | | | | | $ 129. MIL | $ 9. MIL |

KEY :

| P/M $ size | Comp intensity |
|---|---|
| P/M growth | Accessibility |
| P/M share | Margins |
| P&S $ | Our est. 05 sale |

**Figure 5.3**   Product/market matrix: plastics equipment manufacturer.

This company's product/market matrix is basically a 3 × 2 matrix resulting in six potential business opportunities. Product lines consisted of dryers, conveyers, and blenders, three types of equipment that are necessary in the manufacture of plastics products. In each case there were two subcategories of each product. Segmentation was a more difficult process. Ultimately it was decided that plastics manufacturers could be broken down into two types: those who employed low-tech approaches and those who applied high-tech approaches. This segmentation approach was decided upon because salespeople could clearly identify which manufacturers were applying which approach. This certainly satisfies the "findable" requirement for a good segmentation scheme. Further, they all agreed that manufacturers' buying behaviors varied depending on whether they were a low-tech or high-tech manufacturer.

The strategic criteria applied to the matrix consisted of the following:

- Product/market size in dollar potential

- Product/market growth rate

- Competitive intensity of the product/market

- Product/market share

- Accessibility of the product/market

- Product/market margins

Because this organization had not analyzed its business in terms of these markets before, the financial reporting systems could not immediately provide the necessary data for each cell. Data relevant to the selected criteria were available by product line, however, and the management team was able to "back into" the relevant markets well enough for priorities to become evident. With the exception of market size, the actual data has been replaced with approximations.

Applying these criteria uniformly across the matrix led the management team to focus on dehumidifying dryers in the low-tech market and vacuum conveyers in the high-tech market. An examination of the matrix will make clear why these two product/markets were chosen. This is where the company chose to focus its resources and efforts. Does that mean that it will ignore the other product/markets? No. It means that the company will continue to serve them, but management will aggressively invest only in those two that represent the best growth opportunities. Future activities may include focusing on other product/markets. This is what is meant by choosing where to compete. Instead of diluting resource allocation across all possible opportunities, it means making a decision as to which opportunities represent the best options for growth and then investing in them.

A more complex product/market matrix is shown in Figure 5.4. This matrix was developed by a large heavy-equipment dealership in Australia.

| | OM | CM | HC | Quarry | Hire | For | L Govt | S Govt | Ag | BC | Marine | Trucking | Warehouse |
|---|---|---|---|---|---|---|---|---|---|---|---|---|---|
| TTT | | | | | | | | | | | | | |
| Farm trac | | | | | | | | | | | | | |
| Header | | | | | | | | | | | | | |
| MG | | | | | | | | | | | | | |
| HEX | | | | | | | | | | | | | |
| ADT | | | | | | | | | | | | | |
| Compactor | | | | | | | | | | | | | |
| TL | | | | | | | | | | | | | |
| WL | | | | | | | | | | | | | |
| IT | | | | | | | | | | | | | |
| BHL | | | | | | | | | | | | | |
| Skid | | | | | | | | | | | | | |
| Scraper | | | | | | | | | | | | | |
| OHT | | | | | | | | | | | | | |
| Lift truck | | | | | | | | | | | | | |
| Engine | | | | | | | | | | | | | |

**Figure 5.4**   Product/market matrix: heavy-equipment dealership.

Markets are arrayed across the top and product lines are shown on the vertical axis. After assessing its product lines sold and market segments served, this organization found that it had a total of 208 potential business opportunities. This surfaced the realization that it would be impossible to invest equally into all of these different product/markets. After all, how could any organization effectively compete in 208 different product/markets? During this analysis it was also realized that a number of these different opportunities, on their face, were not really viable. For example, owner miners (OM) do not typically buy farm tractors and the marine market doesn't buy hydraulic excavators (HEX). The state governments (S Gov) market may buy the occasional track loader (TL), but this business is really inconsequential. All such nonviable markets were immediately eliminated from consideration. Reviewing sales records and incorporating the views of salespeople and marketers can help identify these nonviable cells.

Due to the large number of potential business opportunities (product/markets), this management team elected to first evaluate the potential among the markets served. Using a variant of the GE portfolio approach, the team evaluated each market in terms of two factors: the attractiveness of each market and the firm's ability to compete effectively in each market, both of which were defined by the management team. Market attractiveness was rated by the management team in terms of the criteria listed in Table 5.1.

The organization's ability to compete was rated in terms of the criteria listed in Table 5.2. The management team collectively determined the relative weights for each criterion, and then each manager individually assigned a rating to each criterion. The average rating score times the relevant weight produced the weighted average score. The markets were then plotted on a matrix based on those weighted averages, as shown in Figure 5.5 on page 59. The matrix ranges from a 1 (low ability to compete or low attractiveness) to a high of 10 (strong ability to compete or high attractiveness).

**Table 5.1**  Market attractiveness.

| Market Attractiveness | Weight | Score | Weighted Score |
|---|---|---|---|
| Size<br>  New/Used/Rental<br>  Total $ size<br>  Total industry—not just where we currently<br>    compete | | | |
| Growth rate<br>  Overall market growth—up, down, flat<br>  Use "5" for average growth (currently<br>    about XX%)<br>  "10" = Much more than average growth<br>  1" = Lower than average or decline | | | |
| Intensity of competition<br>  Number of competitors<br>  Competitive "ferocity" | | | |
| Downstream P/S consumption<br>  Both parts and service<br>  Not just what we capture, total p/s required<br>    because of usage | | | |
| Investment requirement<br>  Consider additional investment required to<br>    compete effectively<br>  Includes people, plant, facilities, info systems,<br>    training<br>  1 = High investment<br>  10 = Low investment | | | |
| Legal/Regulatory/Liability/Environment<br>  1 = Lots of rules and regulations<br>  10 = Few rules and regulations | | | |
| Product specifications/customization<br>  1 = Lots of customization<br>  10 = Little customization | | | |
| Accessibility<br>  10 = Few major customers, easy to identify<br>    and easy to reach | | | |
| Profitability/Initial sale | | | |

Markets in the three cells with vertical lines are clearly high priorities. These are markets that are average-to-outstanding in attractiveness, in which the organization has an average-to-outstanding ability to compete. For opposite reasons, markets in the three cells with horizontal lines should clearly receive no further investment. Although the dealership will continue to serve these markets, it will not invest limited resources in them. The cells on the diagonal required additional quantitative analysis, resulting in the decision

**Table 5.2**   Ability to compete.

| Ability to Compete | Weight | Score | Weighted Score |
|---|---|---|---|
| People<br>  Knowledge of customer's business<br>  Technical expertise<br>  Availability (do we have enough; in all areas)<br>  Managerial ability<br>  Stability/turnover | | | |
| Product<br>  Warranty<br>  Performance<br>  Life cycle/durability<br>  Literal availability (all products for market)<br>  Reliability<br>  Used equipment | | | |
| Product support<br>  Operator training<br>  Service training<br>  Warranty<br>  Delivery times<br>  Parts<br>  Workshop<br>  Field service | | | |
| Organizational<br>  Branch location<br>  Coverage<br>  Cross-functional market focus<br>  Size/bureaucracy<br>  Market-based structure | | | |
| Financial<br>  Cost efficient<br>  Cash flow<br>  Accessible financing<br>  Price<br>  Rental<br>  Trading ability | | | |
| Current market presence<br>  Market share<br>  Visibility | | | |

to include heavy construction (HC) and building construction (BC) among the priorities for investment.

Transferring this information to the business's product/market matrix, shown in Figure 5.6, provided considerable clarity regarding strategic priorities. Product/market cells without lines or dots were eliminated from further consideration because these were deemed nonviable. Product/markets with

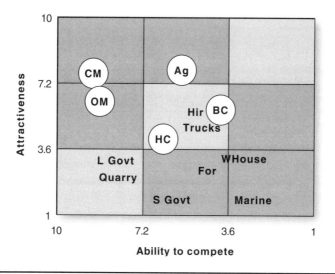

**Figure 5.5**  Market segment investment matrix.

| | OM | CM | HC | Quarry | Hire | For | L Govt | S Govt | Ag | BC | Marine | Trucking | Warehouse |
|---|---|---|---|---|---|---|---|---|---|---|---|---|---|
| TTT | ‖‖‖‖‖‖ | | | | | | | | | | | | |
| Farm trac | | | | | | | | | X | | | | |
| Header | | | | | | | | | X | | | | |
| MG | | | | | | | | | | | | | |
| HEX | X | X | X | | | | | | | X | | | |
| ADT | ‖‖‖‖‖‖ | | | | | | | | | | | | |
| Compactor | | | | | | | | | | | | | |
| TL | | | | | | | | | | | | | |
| WL | ‖‖‖‖‖ | | X | | | | | | ‖‖‖ | | | | |
| IT | | | | | | | | | | | | | |
| BHL | ‖‖‖‖‖ | | | | | | | | ‖‖‖ | X | | | |
| Skid | | | | | | | | | | | | | |
| Scraper | | | | | | | | | | | | | |
| OHT | X | X | | | | | | | | | | | |
| Lift truck | | | | | | | | | ‖‖‖ | | | | |
| Engine | ‖‖‖‖‖‖ | | | | | | | | ‖‖‖ | | | | |

**Figure 5.6**  Heavy-equipment dealer's priorities.

vertical lines or dots were then further evaluated in terms of dollar opportunity, market share, profitability, downstream product support, and so forth, resulting in the identification of 10 strategic priorities, identified with *X*'s.

This analysis reduced the total number of opportunities from 208 to 10. These 10 product/markets represent the arenas in which this organization has chosen to compete. Instead of pumping limited resources into opportunities with marginal value and marginal potential for success, the organization has identified those that can provide the best basis for future growth. It is in these specific product/markets that the organization will concentrate its efforts and resources while continuing to serve the other, less fertile opportunities.

| Segment<br>Product | Singles | Single<br>parents | Full nest<br>1 | Full nest<br>2 | Empty<br>nest | Sole<br>survivor |
|---|---|---|---|---|---|---|
| Savings | | | | | X | X |
| Transaction | X | | | | | |
| Investment | | | | X | | |
| Loans | X | X | X | | | |
| Credit<br>cards | X | | | | | |

**Figure 5.7**　Product/market matrix: financial services.

The segmentation schema used by the equipment dealership was based on the type of application in which its customers worked. This segmentation schema works rather well in that industry, because miners tend to have needs that are considerably different than farmers, who are also considerably different in purchase behaviors from rental companies.

Other industries are better served by different approaches to segmentation. A financial services firm, for example, might segment the market on the basis of life stages, as shown in Figure 5.7.

The commercial bank that uses this matrix has used a life-cycle segmentation approach with the various segments identified across the top of the matrix. The various product lines offered by the bank are arrayed on the vertical axis. Several of these product/markets are nonviable on their face. These would include credit cards to empty nesters or sole survivors, for example. These are eliminated from the start. The strategic criteria used to assess the remaining opportunities included:

- Estimated share of the product/market

- Product/market size

- Product/market growth rate

- Margins

- Cross-selling opportunities to other product/markets

- Product/market ROA

Based on the resulting analysis, the management at this bank determined the top eight priorities for focused competitive investment (identified by *X*'s). These are the competitive arenas in which the bank chose to compete. Each competitive arena has its own competitors, rules for engagement, and success requirements. The very first investment required, of course, was

| Product/market | | Farmers | | | Ag contractors | Ground care | | Landscapers |
|---|---|---|---|---|---|---|---|---|
| | | Full-time | Part-time | Hobby | | Home | Estate | |
| | Lawn | Share　Margins Size/growth PS　　Comp | | | | | | |
| Tractors | Compact | | | | | | | |
| | Mid-sized | | | | | | | |
| | Large | | | | | | | |
| Planters | | | | | | | | |
| Tillage | Plows | | | | | | | |
| | Rippers | | | | | | | |
| | Cultivators | | | | | | | |
| | Disks | | | | | | | |
| Combines | | | | | | | | |
| Harvesters | | | | | | | | |
| Blowers | | | | | | | | |
| Choppers | | | | | | | | |
| Skid steers | | | | | | | | |
| Spreaders | | | | | | | | |
| Balers | Round | | | | | | | |
| | Square | | | | | | | |
| | Wrappers | | | | | | | |
| Mowers | | | | | | | | |
| Windrowers | | | | | | | | |
| Rakes | | | | | | | | |
| Tedders | Mowers | | | | | | | |
| Accessories | Loaders | | | | | | | |
| | PH diggers | | | | | | | |
| | Snowblowers | | | | | | | |
| | Brooms | | | | | | | |
| | Telehandlers | | | | | | | |

*Third dimension: Dealer 1, Dealer 2, And so forth...*

**Figure 5.8** Aligning national and local competitive opportunities.

the research necessary to determine the existing value proposition within that product/market. The successful competitor will want to understand these product/markets better than its competitors. For all the organization's puzzling over the complexities of multibrand strategies, the product/market matrix is a tool that can bring much needed clarity to competitive efforts.

A final example, provided in Figure 5.8, reveals how a manufacturer of farm equipment uses the product/market matrix to link competitive focus at the manufacturer level with competitive focus at the local, dealer level. Dealers had long complained that the manufacturer's competitive focus was not always consistent with that of a specific dealer. By constructing a three-dimensional matrix, with dealers on the third dimension, the manufacturer was able to resolve this conflict. The manufacturer identified strategic priorities at a national level, then drilled those down through the dealer network to reveal which dealers would capitalize on Priority A, which on Priority B, and so forth. Dealer priorities were based on local business opportunities, using the same product/market matrix utilized by the manufacturer at the national level. The aggregate of those local opportunities was then in alignment with national business opportunities.

Clearly, there is no single way in which to develop a product/market matrix, but effective and successful competition requires that the organization be able to identify those specific opportunities that will direct the investment of resources to maximize competitive effectiveness. One of the greatest competitive weaknesses of many organizations is a failure to achieve this kind of focus, which dooms most efforts and resultant strategy deployments to nothing more than an exercise in confusion. The danger of this is most evident in the inability of an organization to clearly articulate its competitive value proposition within a specific product/market. In effect, that organization relinquishes effective control over this highly important asset to its competitors. And, in so doing, the organization loses a key weapon in its ability to increase and sustain its market share position.

The next step is to understand how the product/market defines value and to assess the organization's competitive value proposition for each product/market identified as strategically important. This involves developing a value model, a competitive value matrix, a customer loyalty matrix, and a competitive vulnerability matrix. This is the first resource investment the organization must make if it is to effectively take advantage of the business opportunities identified.

# 6

# What is the Organization's Current Value Proposition?

Once the organization has decided *where* it will compete, it must then address the question of *how* it will compete. Because value is the best predictor of market share and represents a controllable element that can be managed for profitable increases in market share, it simply makes good sense to compete on the basis of superior value creation and delivery. Effectively competing on the basis of value, however, requires the organization to address four specific value questions:

- Strategically, what is your current value proposition?

- What do you want your value proposition to be?

- How do you manage/change your value proposition?

- Do you have/are you progressing toward the value proposition that you intended?

This chapter will address the first question.

## WHAT IS YOUR CURRENT VALUE PROPOSITION?

The answer to this question has four components:

- A value-driver summary

- A competitive value analysis

- An analysis of value strengths and weaknesses

- An identification of market value opportunities

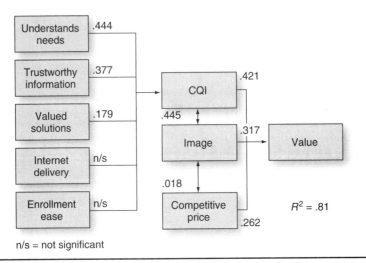

**Figure 6.1** Competitive Value model—disability insurance/large businesses.

## A Value-Driver Summary

The value-driver summary is provided by the value model. The value model shown in Figure 6.1 represents a strategically important product/market identified by an insurance company. It is a value model for disability insurance targeted to larger-sized businesses.

Five quality factors were identified: "understands needs," "trustworthy information," "valued solutions," "Internet delivery," and "enrollment ease." Only three of these are quality drivers: "understands needs," "trustworthy information," and "valued solutions." These are the factors that have the weights next to them. The other two, "Internet delivery" and "enrollment ease," do not factor into the model. From a regression standpoint they are not significant (n/s). Does this mean that they are also unimportant? Not necessarily. One explanation for quality factors that don't enter a regression model is that there is little variability among competitors on these factors. This is also true of factors that are qualifiers, or "table stakes." Qualifiers represent a special kind of market need, or quality component. They are "must haves," and do not currently represent any differentiating capability at the present time. However, failure to perform on a qualifier within any product/market means that any penetration into that market is inhibited. In that sense, qualifiers can act as a significant drag factor. It is imperative to qualify for any targeted product/market that is singled out as an important growth opportunity for the organization.

Price often acts as a qualifier. If a supplier's price is outside the market's acceptable price range, that supplier will probably not be considered for business. It will not be part of the buyer's evoked set. This often happens in consumer situations where the buyer does not consider a company's brand because of the cost, either real or perceived. Other types of qualifiers might include the level of awareness for a brand or inability to comply with specific government or legal restrictions. If large parts of the market are not aware of the brand, then there is little likelihood that buyers would even consider it.

Laws and regulations can often create qualifiers, or cause the precise nature of qualifiers to evolve. For example, if a manufacturer of heavy equipment does not conform to specific noise-abatement regulations, contractors working in populated areas governed by those regulations may not consider that manufacturer's equipment for purchase.

If qualifiers represent one type of market need, differentiators represent another. Differentiators are represented by the value drivers in the models, and more specifically, by the quality drivers on the far left of the models. These are the quality drivers with "importance weights" attached to them. For example, "understands needs" is the most important of the three, followed by "trustworthy information" and then "valued solutions." The relative contributions to quality are shown to the right of each driver in terms of the weights. Solid performance on these quality drivers is essential to achieve a differential value advantage, and the relative weights on each of these drivers will become important in the identification of opportunities, and ultimately in the development of a competitive strategy.

To summarize, the predictive component of the model indicates that quality (CQI) is the most important driver followed by image and then price. On the managerial side of the model, "understands needs" is the number-one quality driver, followed by "trustworthy information" and "valued solutions."

# COMPETITIVE VALUE ANALYSIS

How does the value model transition into a strategic radar screen to reveal the current competitive value propositions of the key suppliers? This is done by way of the competitive value matrix shown in Figure 6.2.

In this case, Company XYZ is located within the "expensive relationship" quadrant based on customer evaluations of its higher-than-market-average quality (CQI) and its less-than-average price satisfaction. In other words, customers indicate that XYZ's offering has a higher-than-average level of quality, but they are not satisfied with its price.

Competitor 1 is the outstanding value competitor, and is also the market share leader in this situation. Competitor 2 is viewed as a competitor providing a discount relationship, lower-than-average quality but at a satisfactory price.

Competitors 3, 4, and 5 are located in "no-man's land," a virtual death valley from a value and market share perspective. Failure to move from this competitive value position means continued diminished share and lower profitability.

This matrix details the competitive value propositions of the various competitors as customers in the marketplace view it. This matrix may or

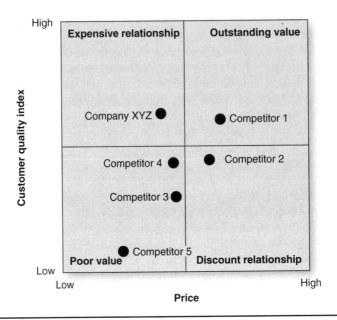

**Figure 6.2** Competitive value matrix—disability insurance/large businesses.

may not coincide with an internal perspective, but it is certainly not arrived at from an internal perspective, which is often little more than a guess. This matrix represents the "voice of the customer" and it provides an important input into how the organization must compete in order to hold onto and win additional customers.

# VALUE STRENGTHS AND WEAKNESSES

By analyzing the organization's value strengths and value weaknesses, management can begin to formulate the necessary components of an effective competitive strategy. The individual head-to-heads for both drivers and specific attributes provide valuable insight into the organization's competitive value proposition.

## Driver-Level Analysis

The first level of analysis of an organization's strengths and weaknesses is done at the driver level. The competitive value matrix reveals relative competitive positions vis-à-vis quality and price, but an analysis of the specific market ratings on each driver reveals whether the differences observed are "real" (statistically significant), and further breaks down the quality driver into is driver components. These differences are shown in Table 6.1.

**Table 6.1**   Head-to-head driver analysis.

|  | Company XYZ | Competitor 1 | Competitor 2 | Competitor 3 | Competitor 4 | Competitor 5 |
|---|---|---|---|---|---|---|
| | | | | Disability benefits provider | | |
| CQI | 7.59 | 7.65 | 7.30 | 7.07 | 7.23 | 6.15 |
| Understands needs | 7.84 | 7.89 | 7.57 | 7.20 | 7.32 | 6.10 |
| Trustworthy information | 7.50 | 7.70 | 7.20 | 6.95 | 7.15 | 6.23 |
| Valued solutions | 7.17 | 6.94 | 6.83 | 6.98 | 7.18 | 6.08 |
| Image | 8.16 | 7.65 | 7.70 | 8.19 | 7.68 | 7.29 |
| Price | 7.33 | 7.93 | 7.77 | 7.31 | 7.39 | 6.57 |

☐ **XYZ advantage**   ☐ **XYZ parity**   ▨ **XYZ disadvantage**

Table 6.1 provides comparisons of performance ratings on the value and quality drivers for the key competitors. These are performance ratings with a 1 = poor performance and a 10 = superior performance. Because Company XYZ is the focus of the competitive analysis, all strengths and weaknesses are indicated relative to Company XYZ. Light gray shaded cells indicate areas where XYZ has an advantage. Dark gray cells represent disadvantages, or weaknesses, for XYZ. Unmarked cells reflect parity between XYZ and the associated competitor. Although scores between XYZ and associated competitors may appear to be different, statistical analyses reveal no real differences, hence parity.

Based on this analysis, Company XYZ enjoys a quality advantage over Competitors 2, 3, 4, and 5, as well as an image advantage over Competitors 1, 4, and 5. XYZ dominates Competitor 5 on all drivers except for price. XYZ also has an advantage over Competitors 3 and 4 on "understands needs," and an advantage over Competitors 2 and 3 on "trustworthy information." XYZ does have a weakness on price relative to Competitor 1. On all other drivers, XYZ and its competitors are at parity.

## VPC-Level Analysis

The driver level of analysis provides some general direction for competitive planning, but if your organization's competitive plans are to be truly effective, they will need to be directive at a more granular level. The individual VPCs (value performance criteria), or questionnaire items, that comprise the drivers, as shown in Table 6.2, provide that granularity.

**Table 6.2** Driver VPCs for disability insurance.

| Factors and attributes |
| --- |
| **Internet delivery** |
| Providing online transactional abilities |
| Providing user-friendly Internet access |
| Providing accurate and secure Web transactions |
| Offering multiple means of access for managers |
| Providing your employees with easy access |
| Educating employees in person or via the Internet |
| **Understands needs** |
| Minimizing paperwork |
| Providing easy-to-understand reports |
| Having easy-to-understand pricing policies |
| Accuracy of charges |
| Having easy-to-follow claims procedures |
| Having easy-to-follow administrative procedures |
| Providing error-free reporting of information |
| Making your job easier |
| Keeping you informed of plan changes |
| Handling administrative issues quickly and accurately |
| **Trustworthy information** |
| Not changing reps too frequently |
| Providing local access to an advisor |
| Using agents who know about you and your needs |
| Offering frequent personal contact |
| Having well-informed agents |
| Making it easy to contact agents over time |
| Understanding your business, needs, and solutions |
| Creating trusting relationships |
| Building long-lasting relationships with customers |
| Providing end-to-end solutions |

The comparison of mean ratings for XYZ and its competitors on the VPCs underlying the "understands needs" quality driver is shown in Table 6.3. As in Table 6.1, statistically significant strengths and weaknesses for XYZ relative to each competitor are shown with dots or lines, respectively.

The "understands needs" driver provides an illustration of how this decomposition works. The "understands needs" driver is comprised of the individual VPCs listed under it. Company XYZ enjoys an advantage over Competitor 5 on the driver as well as on 9 of its 10 constituent

**Table 6.2** Driver VPCs for disability insurance. (*continued*)

| Factors and attributes |
| --- |
| **Valued solutions** |
| Offering customization of plans to your business |
| Offering customization of plans to your employees |
| Offering custom plans |
| **Enrollment ease** |
| Providing help in enrolling employees |
| Providing for easy enrollment of employees |
| **Value** |
| Providing services that are worth what you pay for them |
| Providing good service for the price that you pay |
| Rate value you receive on a scale of 1 to 10 |
| **Price** |
| Competitive price |
| Fair price |
| Best price |
| **Image** |
| Enjoying favorable name recognition |
| Having a reputable image |
| Being a provider that is recognized by employees |
| Having an excellent reputation |
| Demonstrating that it is financially stable |
| Demonstrating honesty in all of its dealings |
| Keeping up with innovative changes in the industry |

VPCs. Regarding Competitor 4, XYZ enjoys an advantage on the driver and 3 of the 10 VPCs. XYZ has an advantage over Competitor 3 on the driver and on five attributes and a single advantage over Competitor 2. With regard to Competitor 1, XYZ's major competitor and market share leader, XYZ is at parity on both the driver level and on all constituent attributes.

These head-to-head comparisons provide the strategic fuel to power competitive efforts to change an organization's competitive value proposition. If XYZ wants to increase its market share position within this product/market (disability insurance for large businesses) it must enhance its competitive value proposition relative to that of Competitor 1, in particular. And to do this, it must understand how to change its performance scores on key drivers and the individual attributes that constitute the drivers.

**Table 6.3** Strengths and weaknesses at the VPC level.

| | Disability benefits provider | | | | | |
|---|---|---|---|---|---|---|
| | Company XYZ | Competitor 1 | Competitor 2 | Competitor 3 | Competitor 4 | Competitor 5 |
| Understands needs | 7.85 | 7.92 | 7.57 | 7.20 | 7.27 | 6.14 |
| Minimizing paperwork | 7.54 | 7.89 | 6.84 | 7.40 | 6.94 | 6.31 |
| Providing easy-to-understand reports | 7.88 | 7.69 | 7.40 | 7.16 | 7.45 | 5.75 |
| Having easy-to-understand pricing policies | 7.92 | 8.13 | 7.78 | 7.28 | 7.08 | 6.31 |
| Accuracy of charges | 8.49 | 8.00 | 8.06 | 8.00 | 7.71 | 6.31 |
| Having easy-to-follow claims procedures | 7.63 | 8.20 | 7.76 | 7.26 | 7.18 | 6.71 |
| Having easy-to-follow administrative procedures | 7.86 | 7.94 | 7.68 | 7.30 | 7.41 | 6.25 |
| Providing error-free reporting of information | 7.83 | 7.89 | 7.70 | 7.28 | 7.34 | 6.13 |
| Making your job easier | 7.56 | 7.52 | 7.11 | 6.35 | 6.96 | 5.63 |
| Keeping you informed of plan changes | 8.07 | 8.23 | 7.97 | 7.26 | 7.20 | 6.20 |
| Handling administrative issues quickly and accurately | 7.72 | 7.68 | 7.39 | 6.75 | 7.43 | 5.81 |

☐ XYZ advantage    ☐ XYZ parity    ▨ XYZ disadvantage

# IDENTIFICATION OF MARKET OPPORTUNITIES

Successful and efficient competition for customers involves the identification of specific and actionable market opportunities. Too often market opportunities are the stuff of imagination and agendas. They come from nowhere and have no apparent linkage to the actual situation in the marketplace. Identifying market opportunities is a disciplined and logical process that flows directly from what customers are telling you about the competitive value propositions of the key product or service providers in that product/market. The matrix shown in Figure 6.3 provides a systematic process for identifying and prioritizing customer-driven market opportunities.

The first place any organization should look to identify market opportunities is the cell pertaining to qualifiers on which the organization may have a weakness. Qualifiers are "must haves," and failure to qualify retards penetration and operates as a drag factor. In the current example, if XYZ has

| | Customers' qualifying needs: value screening equation | Customers' determining needs: value decision equation |
|---|---|---|
| Company strength: value advantage | | (2) Leverage for differential value advantage |
| Competitive parity | | (3) Enhance to achieve value advantage |
| Company weakness: value disadvantage | (1) Critical to qualify for consideration | (4) Improve if related need is important |

**Figure 6.3** Value opportunity identification matrix.

a weakness on a qualifier, it must address this weakness if it wishes to participate fully in the business opportunity afforded by this product/market (selling disability insurance to large businesses). However, there is no evidence that XYZ fails to qualify for consideration in this product/market. The company enjoys high levels of market awareness, is readily accessible by large businesses, enjoys a reputation for financial stability, and has performance ratings equivalent to the competition on the two quality factors that did not load into the value model ("Internet delivery" and "enrollment ease"). Consequently, XYZ management can move on to the next potential source of opportunity, a strength on a determining need (driver). It should be noted that a strength or parity on a qualifier does not represent a potential opportunity, all things being equal. By definition, the organization either qualifies for consideration or it does not. Further investment into areas where the organization already qualifies would be wasteful, though each organization must be mindful that it retains its qualifying position.

Organizations get much more competitive bang for their dollar by investing in an opportunity that is defined as a strength on a driver, as shown by priority 2 on the opportunity matrix. Leveraging value advantages, especially important value advantages (indicated by the relative weight of the driver), provides a strong strategic force to drive increases in market share. The value model identifies with precision the relative importance of all drivers. Strengths on the most important drivers can be leveraged into profitable market share gains.

Many managers think that leveraging a strength means simply putting together a communication strategy that touts the organization's recognized strength on a given driver. Although communication will often be involved in any leveraging strategy, truly leveraging a strength on a quality driver typically requires more than that if that value advantage is to be sustainable over the long term. Caterpillar (CAT), for example, recognized its distribution system—its dealer network—as a differentiating strength in the 1980s. Customers in every market in which CAT chose to compete recognized the value that CAT dealers provided relative to key competitors such as Komatsu, Volvo, John Deere, and others. The simplistic way to "leverage" that strength would have been for Caterpillar to increase advertising with a focus on dealer sales and service. CAT's North American management, however, recognized that to truly leverage its dealer network meant to help those dealers become even better—more attuned to market dynamics and more capable of creating and delivering superior value. Accordingly, CAT's management embarked on a substantial dealer development program designed to make dealers stronger and impregnable to competitive intrusion by Komatsu, Case, or other competitors. This dealer strength continues to differentiate the huge heavy-equipment manufacturer and continues to thwart strategic efforts of competitors to gain share on CAT.

The third source of potential market opportunity resides in the intersection of competitive parity with determining needs, but only if such parity exists with respect to the targeted competitor. Referring back to Figure 6.2, Company, XYZ's targeted competitor would be Competitor 1. To the extent that XYZ is at parity with Competitor 1 on key drivers, to that extent XYZ is in a strong position to enhance performance on those drivers, resulting in a clear differential advantage. This is particularly effective when an organization finds itself competing against an inexperienced competitor, or one that has no experience competing on a value basis.

The final source for market opportunities occurs when an organization has a weakness on a value driver. Improving on a value differentiator, especially on an important one, will probably be necessary for sustained value differentiation. In fact, if an organization has a weakness on the most important quality driver and a strength on the least important quality driver, the former would likely rise to become a higher priority than the latter.

Using this approach to identify market value opportunities, XYZ would first evaluate whether there were any qualifying issues. Having determined that XYZ has no weaknesses on qualifiers, management would then turn to any strengths or parity positions it had relative to Competitor 1, its most serious threat. Logic dictates a focus on the quality (CQI) drivers because quality is the most important driver of value in this product/market, price is a relatively unimportant source of value differentiation, and image is a longer-term source of differentiation that is also strongly related to quality ($r = .445$). In other words, as quality improves, the organization's image ratings will follow.

Table 6.1 reveals no competitive strengths for XYZ versus Competitor 1. XYZ is at parity with Competitor 1 on all quality drivers, meaning that XYZ has an opportunity to enhance performance on these drivers to achieve a competitive advantage, which can then be leveraged into greater market share. Proceeding on a priority basis, the first opportunity for XYZ pertains to the "understands needs" quality driver. Further examination of strengths and weaknesses on the attributes underlying this driver would yield the following opportunity:

*To enhance and leverage our ability to understand customer needs by emphasizing:*

1. *XYZ's ability to minimize paperwork*

2. *Easy-to-understand reports*

3. *Easy-to-understand pricing policies*

4. *Accuracy of charges*

These are the issues that human resources (HR) and benefit managers in large businesses identified as defining "understands needs." Leveraging may mean taking advantage of this opportunity through communication messages targeted at HR people and benefits managers through advertising, sales channels, or direct mail. But, it may also mean investing in those processes that lead to the minimization of paperwork and enhancing the reporting process. This assures that XYZ will, at the very least, stay at parity, but more than likely turn its parity position into an actual value advantage on the number-one value driver.

Another opportunity for XYZ, and second among priorities, pertains to the second quality driver trustworthy information and its attributes:

*To enhance and leverage the trustworthiness of our information by:*

1. *Retaining quality sales reps with consistent client assignments*

2. *Providing local access to advisors*

3. *Providing frequent personal contact*

4. *Making it easy for clients to contact us*

XYZ's third priority pertaining to quality drivers valued solution would be:

*To enhance and leverage our ability to provide customized solutions, such as:*

1. *Providing plans that are customized to the client's business*

2. *Providing plan customization for different employee groups*

At the same time, XYZ has an actual advantage on the image driver. Although XYZ's image will be enhanced through the enhancement of performance on the quality drivers themselves, the relatively high contribution of the image driver to value suggests another opportunity for organizational focus:

*To leverage XYZ's industry-recognized image by emphasizing:*

1. *Favorable name recognition*

2. *Reputation*

3. *Recognition by employees*

This opportunity may entail mostly a promotional thrust.

Finally, XYZ has a disadvantage to Competitor 1 on pricing. The model does not reveal whether this advantage is perceptual or actual. However, a literal comparison of price points will reveal whether the opportunity is one of correcting existing market perceptions or one of modifying the organization's pricing strategy. In either event, the opportunity exists for XYZ:

*To enhance or improve its pricing policies.*

In all cases, the value-enhancing opportunity is stated at the driver level, and illustrated or fleshed out at the attribute level. This ensures that opportunities are prioritized in terms of value drivers, and that sufficient detail is included for each opportunity to ensure high levels of actionability and the capacity to actually drive strategy.

Organizations using a systematic process like this to identify existing opportunities can be assured that their resulting strategies will be value based and focused on market-driven priorities. Whether all opportunities identified through this process will be incorporated in the competitive strategy for the targeted product/market will be a function of several other considerations, including the nature of the business unit's objectives and their relative priority. Two considerations, in particular, will help determine priorities within the strategy: customer acquisition and customer retention, which both result in profitable increases in market share.

# CUSTOMER ACQUISITION

One source of increased market share is the customer base of each competitor in the targeted product/market. Some or all of the market opportunities identified by linking market needs with the organization's competitive strengths and weaknesses will ultimately become part of the organization's strategy to compete effectively in this product/market. But an examination of specific competitor vulnerabilities will enable the organization to place appropriate emphasis on those opportunities that will most effectively exploit specific competitors. In other words, some of the opportunities identified will be particularly effectively in picking the "low-hanging fruit" from the competition.

The competitor vulnerability matrix shown in Figure 6.4 illustrates customers of XYZ's competitors grouped on the basis of the value they perceive

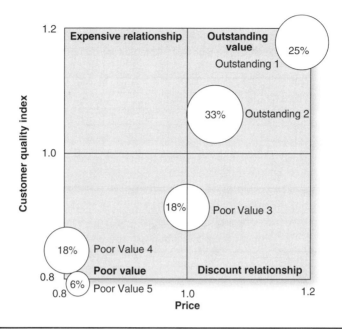

**Figure 6.4**   Competitor vulnerability matrix—disability insurance/large businesses.

as being received from their insurance provider. The competitor vulnerability matrix is developed in the same manner as the competitive value matrix, with the CQI on the vertical axis and price satisfaction on the horizontal axis. The difference is that instead of locating competitors on the matrix, the competitor vulnerability matrix plots groups of competitors' customers based on scores for the CQI and price satisfaction. The larger the circle, the larger the group of customers.

In this case, 25 percent of all competitors' customers report that they are receiving truly outstanding value from their provider, and another 33 percent report that they are receiving somewhat outstanding value. These 58 percent of competitor customers are pretty firmly entrenched with their current provider, and will be fairly resistant to competitive intrusion from XYZ. Groups 3, 4, and 5, representing 42 percent of all competitor customers, are either passively or actively willing to consider alternatives.

Table 6.4 reveals the distribution of competitor customers by value group. Two competitors have significant vulnerabilities that might be exploited. Forty-two percent of Competitor 3's customers are located in Poor Value Group 3, and 43 percent of competitor 5's customers are located in Poor Value Group 4. Nearly half the customers of those two competitors are ready, if not eager, to consider alternative providers. Tables 6.5 and 6.6 reveal the bases of those vulnerabilities.

Based on these analyses, a competitive strategy that includes the market opportunity to "enhance and leverage the trustworthiness of information" will

**Table 6.4** Competitor vulnerabilities.

|  | Competitor 1 | Competitor 2 | Competitor 3 | Competitor 4 | Competitor 5 |
|---|---|---|---|---|---|
| **Outstanding 1** | 28.9% | 27.8% | 10.5% | 26.4% | 21.4% |
| **Outstanding 2** | 37.8% | 27.8% | 31.6% | 37.7% | 7.1% |
| **Poor 3** | 11.1% | 30.6% | (42.1%) | 11.3% | 7.1% |
| **Poor 4** | 17.8% | 8.3% | 15.6% | 18.9% | (42.9%) |
| **Poor 5** | 4.4% | 5.6% |  | 5.7% | 21.4% |

**Table 6.5** Quality driver performance ratings—Competitor 3.

| Competitor 3 | Value group 1 | Value group 2 | Value group 3 | Value group 4 | Value group 5 |
|---|---|---|---|---|---|
| **Understands needs\*** | 9.90 | 8.51 | 6.63 | 4.60 | 3.36 |
| **Trustworthy information** | 9.40 | 7.52 | (5.41) | 5.90 | 4.60 |
| **Valued solutions** | 9.83 | 6.83 | 6.69 | 5.56 | 4.02 |

\*10 = outstanding performance, 1 = poor performance

**Table 6.6** Quality driver performance ratings—Competitor 5.

| Competitor 5 | Value group 1 | Value group 2 | Value group 3 | Value group 4 | Value group 5 |
|---|---|---|---|---|---|
| **Understands needs\*** | 9.17 | 6.30 | 6.60 | 5.49 | 2.93 |
| **Trustworthy information** | 8.93 | 7.40 | 6.67 | 5.80 | 3.43 |
| **Valued solutions** | 9.67 | 9.71 | 6.50 | (4.23) | 3.44 |

\*10 = outstanding performance, 1 = poor performance

be particularly effective among customers of Competitor 3, and a strategy that includes the market opportunity to "enhance and leverage the ability to provide customized solutions" will be very effective with customers of Competitor 5. In other words, in addition to being market-driven opportunities to provide value differentiation on a broad basis, capitalizing on these two opportunities will be particularly effective for the purpose of customer acquisition, especially from Competitors 3 and 5.

# CUSTOMER RETENTION

The second source of market share growth emanates from the retention of one's own customers. Profitable market share is comprised of acquiring profitable customers while simultaneously retaining profitable customers. A competitive strategy that includes customer retention as a goal

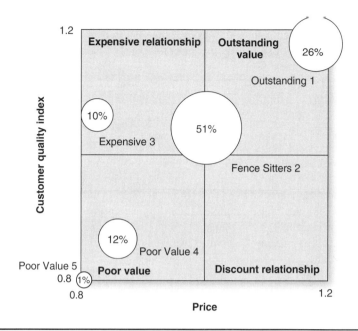

**Figure 6.5** Customer loyalty matrix—XYZ Company.

requires a separate analysis focused on XYZ's current customer base. How loyal are XYZ's customers? To what degree is XYZ vulnerable to competitive intrusion? What is the basis of the vulnerability? Figure 6.5 reveals how five different groups of XYZ's customers perceive the value that they currently receive.

The customer loyalty matrix is constructed in the same manner as the competitor vulnerability matrix, except that this time the customer groups are XYZ's current customers. The customer loyalty matrix identifies the degree to which XYZ's customer base is loyal and the basis of that loyalty. From another perspective, the matrix identifies the degree to which XYZ's customer base is vulnerable and on what basis that vulnerability exists.

Twenty-six percent of XYZ's customers are located within the "outstanding value" quadrant and represent the most loyal customers within the base. These are the customers that are most likely to recommend XYZ to other customers and least likely to defect under price pressures.

Fifty-one percent of XYZ's customers are somewhat loyal customers, indicating that they are getting average value. They are passive shoppers with a certain number of them willing to seek other insurance suppliers when their contracts expire. Clearly, their position on the matrix could be better, in that the centroid of the cluster could be located higher and to the right within the "outstanding value" quadrant. The further toward the upper-right corner of the matrix, the stronger the loyalty of the group. A strategic goal would be to move these customers toward the other group (Group 1) of outstanding value customers.

Ten percent of XYZ's customer base is located within the "expensive relationship" quadrant, indicating that though this group of customers is getting high quality, they perceive that quality is coming at a price that is less than satisfactory.

Two groups of customers are located within the "poor value" quadrant, and they are highly vulnerable to competitive intrusion. One group comprises 12 percent of XYZ's customer base while the other group comprises 1 percent.

The matrix is a valuable tool for understanding the dynamics of retention. In this insurance example, each customer group can be profiled in terms of such factors as annual sales, premiums, contract renewal, complaints, billing inquiries, service costs, payouts, and so on. In other cases these groups can be profiled regarding product support revenues, repair revenues, warranty costs, parts revenues, and so on. This information is vital in determining the exact management strategy for handling these different groups of customers. For example, looking at the 1 percent of customers in the poor value group located at the bottom of the matrix, depending on their profiles, it may be better (depending on how profitable this group of customers is) to harvest these customers and not spend a lot of money trying to keep them as customers. If they are unprofitable, they are a drag on XYZ's profitability and, as such, few resources should be spent on their retention.

A second inquiry should focus on what individual or systemic factors account for the varying levels of value that these customers are receiving. Looking at the group of customers that constitutes 51 percent of XYZ's customer base, it is important to understand what dynamics are operating here. Are there any systemic factors associated with these customers? Are there any product-related issues? Distribution or sales issues? Service issues? Firmographic issues (types of companies)? Geographic issues associated with brokers or sales agents? These are the types of issues that, when surfaced, provide important input into the redesign of processes and delivery systems that enhance an organization's competitive value proposition. The individual groups provide a valuable laboratory for failure analysis. Why is XYZ failing to provide the kind of value that creates highly loyal customers impervious to competitive price discounting?

A further analysis of XYZ's performance ratings on quality drivers by customer group, shown in Table 6.7, provides insight into a systemic failure. Of the three quality drivers that make up the CQI, XYZ is rated lowest on "understands needs" by customers in Group 2. An emphasis on this high-priority opportunity, identified earlier in the opportunity analysis, will not only enhance XYZ's overall value proposition, but will also go a long way toward enhancing the loyalty of 51 percent of XYZ's current customer base.

**Table 6.7** XYZ performance ratings by value group.

| XYZ | Value group 1 | Value group 2 | Value group 3 | Value group 4 | Value group 5 |
|---|---|---|---|---|---|
| **Understands needs*** | 9.32 | 6.58 | 8.29 | 5.11 | 2.20 |
| **Trustworthy information** | 9.27 | 7.61 | 7.90 | 4.61 | 2.30 |
| **Valued solutions** | 8.67 | 7.23 | 7.70 | 5.21 | 3.24 |

*10 = outstanding performance, 1 = poor performance

To recap, market opportunities are derived from the matching of an organization's competitive strengths and weaknesses as perceived in the marketplace with the qualifying needs and value differentiators identified in the competitive value model. Organizations with weaknesses on qualifiers must address those first. These are the market opportunities that will enable the organization to play in the game. A failure to identify these opportunities, or a failure to incorporate these opportunities in the competitive strategy for this product/market, will result in a failure to even be considered by any or all of the customers considering this product or service. The second priority in identifying existing opportunities is to match the organization's market-perceived strengths with value drivers, otherwise known as determining needs. Many organizations incorrectly focus on fixing weaknesses rather than on leveraging strengths. This is particularly inappropriate if the organization's strengths are on very important drivers, and the weaknesses are on relatively unimportant drivers. The competitive landscape is littered with companies that invest heavily in fixing insignificant weaknesses while ignoring important strengths. This is also true of companies that tout strengths on relatively unimportant drivers. Priorities are easily determined by relying upon the value model, as defined within the product/market. Finally, if the organization has weaknesses on very important drivers, these also represent opportunities for value enhancement.

Once value opportunities have been identified, a further examination of customer loyalty and competitors' vulnerabilities will provide additional clarification regarding which of these opportunities will be most effective for customer acquisition and which will be most effective for enhancing customer loyalty. This evaluation will be particularly useful when selecting opportunities for inclusion in the organization's competitive strategy, described in the next Chapter.

This is a logical and disciplined approach for achieving and sustaining a differential value advantage. At the heart of this advantage is an outstanding competitive value proposition that cannot be duplicated or neutralized. This represents the first step in addressing the planning question, "How does the organization compete?" Achieving an outstanding competitive value proposition requires a thorough understanding of where the organization currently stands in each of its targeted product/markets. The process described in this Chapter addresses the first of the four planning questions for effective competitive planning:

*What is the organization's current value proposition?*

*What are the key value drivers?*

*What are the firm's strengths and weaknesses?*

*How does the organization stack up against competitors?*

*What are the firm's opportunities?*

Chapter 7 will describe the steps necessary to determine the organization's desired value proposition, and the process of identifying crystal-clear targets for directing competitive action.

# 7

# What Does the Organization Want Its Competitive Value Proposition to Be?

Does the market perceive and understand your competitive value proposition in the same way as you do? Is this the way you want the market to understand your value relative to that of your competitors? If you haven't actively and aggressively been managing your competitive value proposition, the answer to these two questions is "probably not." As we have said before, your competitive value proposition is an extremely important and valuable asset that requires management, just as you manage other organizational assets. And, as we have also pointed out, if you are not actively managing your value proposition, your competition is.

Once the organization has determined how the market actually perceives its competitive value proposition, the next step is to decide what the organization wants its competitive value proposition to be. It is important to keep in mind that the value proposition is directly related to how the *market* defines value, not how *management* defines value. Therefore, the intended value proposition must still rely on the market value information. It is at this point that value and market share come together. Recall that value—market-perceived value—is a strong predictor of market share. A strategy to enhance a value proposition or sustain a value advantage will directly impact the organization's market share.

There are four relevant issues to be addressed for effective management toward the organization's intended value proposition:

1. What are your product/market business objectives?

2. What assumptions underlie these objectives?

3. What competitive strategy will lead to the attainment of those objectives?

4. Which of your existing market opportunities should become part of that strategy?

# PRODUCT/MARKET OBJECTIVES

Product/market objectives are business performance objectives that are usually couched in terms of market share, margins, revenues, unit sales, the organization's competitive value proposition, or some combination of these. Typically, the business objectives for a product/market will parallel the criteria used to identify strategically important product/markets in the first place, as discussed in Chapter 5.

In most cases, the product/market planning team will have market share gain as one of its objectives, although there are occasions when the objective may be to stop market share erosion. The challenge to increasing market share lies in increasing share without decreasing margins. Many enterprises have captured additional share by dropping prices, only to find out that the marginal gains were not profitable. The goal, of course, is to achieve profitable market share gains, which will come through enhancements in the organization's competitive value proposition.

The planning horizon will determine the time frames for product/market objectives. Objectives are typically identified for more than one year, although the idea that an organization can project out to five years or more has been debunked. Nonetheless, market share and other business objectives should be set for two or three years so the organization can track progress toward those objectives and make adjustments where necessary.

Product/market objectives should conform to the basic requirements of all good objectives. They should be specific, reachable, time bound, and, of course, quantifiable (capable of being measured). An example of objectives meeting these criteria is drawn from a distributor of forklifts targeting the warehousing industry:

*P/M objectives:*

- *Increase market share from 18 percent in 2004 to 19 percent by year end 2005, to 23 percent year end 2006, to 28 percent by year end 2007, and to 33 percent by year end 2008, while increasing margins from 11 percent to 14 percent over that time period.*

- *Increase CQI score from 7.89 to 8.85 by year end 2008. Increase price score from 7.41 to 8.0 by 2008. Achieve customer retention rates of 90 percent or higher.*

These objectives conform to all the requirements of good objectives and include not only a market share focus but also a focus on value (CQI and price), customer retention (a critical aspect of market share), and margins. Note also that the product/market objectives are multiyear.

## Assumptions

The organization's business objectives for targeted product/markets are not developed within a vacuum. Each business unit within an organization has specific profitability and cash flow objectives (among others) that will impact the objectives for each targeted product/market, which in turn are impacted by the overall growth objectives of the corporation. Moreover, there are numerous exogenous variables impacting the efficacy of every plan that must be identified and monitored during plan deployment.

Many organizations have some systematic process in place to identify trends that may impact their business plans, whether those trends represent a potential opportunity or a potential threat. This process is typically referred to as "environmental scanning" in the business-planning literature, and includes the monitoring of such things as economic, legal, social, and competitive trends. A brief discussion and several examples from such monitoring systems are provided in Appendix B.

Although it is helpful to identify and monitor trends at the corporate and business-unit levels, such trends will clearly impact assumptions pertaining to objectives and strategies at the product/market level. Based on trends identified and monitored by the forklift planning team, the following assumptions were specifically identified as having potential impact on the product/market objectives and the resulting strategy:

- Total industry growth, while historically high, will diminish from a 30 percent growth rate in 2005, to 20 percent in 2006, to 10 percent in 2007, to 7 percent in 2008

- Cost of materials to produce goods will increase at the rate of 3 percent/year

- Competitors across the board, and especially Competitor 3, are improving in their product support capabilities, potentially eroding an historical strength of XYZ

- Increasing e-commerce will make pricing policies more transparent, and will make used equipment more readily accessible

These assumptions address the various uncontrollable aspects of an organization's competitive reality. Typically they are broken down into economic, competitive, resource and supply, social and cultural, and political/legal factors. In addition, it is useful to identify the consequences of the factors and the time frame in which those consequences are likely to be felt. Examples of useful formats are provided in Appendix C.

# DEVELOP A PRODUCT/MARKET STRATEGY

If you read different business-planning documents it is not uncommon to find strategies that make little, if any, sense in terms of the competitive reality facing the organization. A residual of the dominance of "strategic planning" during the 1970s and 1980s is the *esoterica* that pervaded strategy development. It seemed that the more complex and more erudite the strategy, the better. Not so. The less complex and the more logical a strategy is, the more likely it is to be a winning strategy.

Another key reason that competitive strategies miss their mark is that they are based on internal perspectives of value, rather than on external, market perspectives. Consider, for example, how our forklift distributor thought its targeted market—warehousing customers—would define value, as shown in Figure 7.1.

Based on this internal perspective, a planning team for this product/market might focus first on the organization's pricing policies, followed by a focus on the quality drivers. Their perspective on quality clearly reinforces the manufacturer's claim that the bulk of what drives value resides in the forklift's intrinsic quality and the manufacturer's ability to provide parts quickly. Contrast this with the actual perspective of the warehousing market, as empirically determined, and shown in Figure 7.2.

This misalignment between internal and external definitions of value would clearly cause the organization to emphasize the wrong elements in a competitive strategy. In fact, because the identification of market opportunities is a function of the *interaction* between value (quality drivers) and organizational strengths and weaknesses, the correct identification of relevant opportunities is also a function of the alignment of perspectives on the organization's value proposition. In this case, our forklift distributor saw itself as the clear value leader, as shown in Figure 7.3.

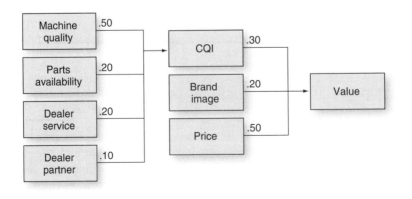

**Figure 7.1** Forklifts/warehouse value model—internal perspective.

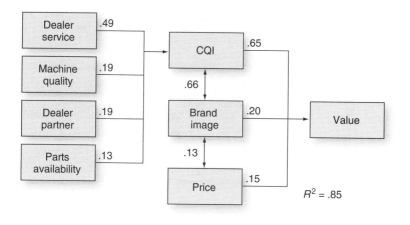

**Figure 7.2**   Forklifts/warehouse value model—market perspective.

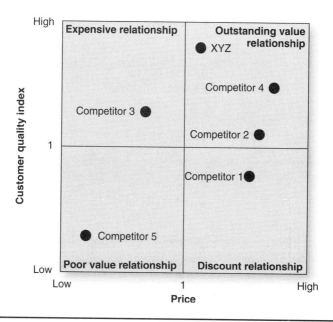

**Figure 7.3**   Forklifts/warehouse value propositions—internal perspective.

This, in contrast with the market's perspective, as shown in Figure 7.4, reveals that warehousing customers perceive no difference among most suppliers with regard to value creation and delivery. This type of comparison, called a "gap analysis," reveals the differences between internal and external perspectives on value creation and delivery. It can be very useful to conduct this sort of gap analysis to make managers aware of the misalignment that frequently exists between the organization's mental model and the mental

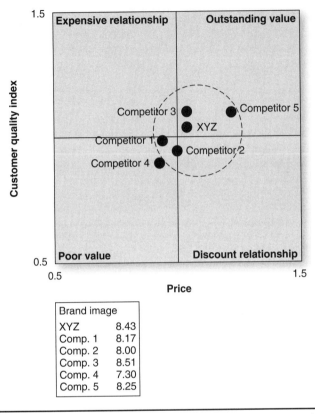

**Figure 7.4**    Forklifts/warehouse value propositions—market perspective.

model that customers use to make purchase decisions. Expect significant and substantial differences in perspectives when the organization is product focused instead of customer or market focused. Clearly, the competitive strategy to emerge from this organization's internal mental model would be very different from the strategy driven by a market perspective.

The organization's strategy for each targeted product/market details and communicates how it will take advantage of the opportunities identified from its analysis of market perspectives on value. The process of opportunity identification was discussed in detail in Chapter 6. Strategy statements are comprised of three parts:

1. The position the organization wants to occupy

2. The target

3. The opportunities

Recall that the main question to be answered at this level of competitive planning is "How does the organization compete?" Therefore, the strategy must ar-

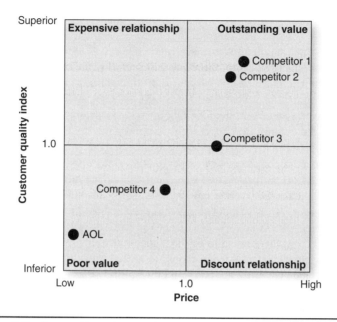

**Figure 7.5** Competitive value matrix—ISP/residential users.

ticulate how the organization will enhance its competitive value proposition in order to achieve profitable increases in market share. Because value is relative, the strategy must articulate the position the organization chooses to occupy relative to a competitor. There are only four basic positions. An organization can:

1. Lead

2. Challenge

3. Follow

4. Niche

The forklift/warehousing competitive value matrix shown in Figure 7.4 reveals that there is no clear value leader at the present time. This is a fairly common situation in a competitive environment in which no supplier has made an effort to compete on the basis of providing superior value. In a value parity situation like this, XYZ's strategy would clearly involve attaining value leadership because value is the best leading indictor of market share, and XYZ's business objective for this product/market is to increase market share while simultaneously increasing profitability.

Suppose, however, that your company were in the position of AOL in a 1999 evaluation of Internet service providers (ISPs) by residential customers, as shown in Figure 7.5. In a competitive situation like this, AOL may well choose to *follow* the value leaders, Competitor 1 or Competitor 2. "Following" requires an acknowledgement on the part of the follower that it cannot match the resource commitment of the leader but does not want the gap to increase. The follower may choose to emulate what the leader is doing but on a smaller resource scale. Of course, a "follower" strategy may result in gradually closing the value gap such that the organization could eventually become a challenger in this product/market.

If Competitor 3 were the focus of the strategy, AOL would probably choose to *challenge* Competitor 1 or 2 for value leadership. Challenging can occur if the organization has a realistic opportunity to close the value differential between itself and the leader. Challenging may take more than one cycle depending on the distance between the competitors.

Organizations may choose to *niche* if they do not have the product line breadth that the other competitors have. They, like KFC, choose to "do chicken right." They will not compete across the board on all fast foods but instead pick something they do well and execute it as well as they can. In the past, nicheing was thought to be the strategy of smaller organizations. But some larger organizations may choose to niche in specific product/markets while competing across the board in others. Firms that "buy to sell" to acquire a presence in a growing market may choose to niche in the short term.

Inherent in the positioning aspect of the strategy is the identification of a competitor. Organizations will choose to lead, challenge, follow, or niche in relation to another competitor. In the case of our forklift distributor, Company XYZ could choose any competitor to target except Competitor 4, since all other competitors are statistically equivalent to XYZ on the basis of value creation and delivery. Based on the actual value driver scores, shown in Table 7.1, XYZ chose to target Competitor 3. This decision was made be-

**Table 7.1** Head-to-head driver analysis—forklifts/warehouse.

| | Company XYZ | Competitor 1 | Competitor 2 | Competitor 3 | Competitor 4 | Competitor 5 |
|---|---|---|---|---|---|---|
| | | | **Lift Truck Company** | | | |
| CQI | 7.89 | 7.74 | 7.54 | 8.47 | 7.22 | 8.32 |
|   Dealer service | 7.69 | 7.20 | 7.01 | 8.35 | 6.93 | 7.41 |
|   Machine quality | 8.26 | 8.27 | 8.32 | 8.48 | 7.84 | 9.09 |
|   Dealer partner | 8.00 | 7.38 | 6.97 | 8.19 | 7.14 | 8.05 |
|   Parts availability | 7.96 | 6.47 | 6.97 | 7.70 | 6.82 | 8.32 |
| Image | 8.43 | 8.17 | 8.00 | 8.51 | 7.30 | 8.25 |
| Price | 7.41 | 6.74 | 7.18 | 7.43 | 6.68 | 8.55 |
| Value | 7.93 | 7.19 | 7.61 | 8.05 | 6.76 | 8.10 |

| | XYZ advantage | | XYZ parity | | XYZ disadvantage |
|---|---|---|---|---|---|

cause the planning team recognized that if they can improve on the quality drivers, they will also improve on price satisfaction due to the high correlation between quality and price ($r = .83$), which in turn should also give them a value advantage over Competitor 5.

XYZ is at parity with Competitor 3 on all the individual value and quality drivers. XYZ does have a disadvantage relative to Competitor 5 on price, has one quality driver—strength—versus Competitors 1 and 2, and has an overall value advantage relative to Competitor 4, based on both quality and image advantages.

The "how" of the strategy comes from identifying the organization's specific market opportunities, based on the interaction of the market's qualifying and determining needs with the organization's specific strengths and weaknesses, as shown in Figure 7.6.

The forklift planning team identified the following qualifiers that could possibly serve as drag factors, preventing them from being considered by some segments of the warehousing market. This information does not necessarily come from the value analysis. Lost sales and refusals may prove to be an important source of information regarding qualifiers.

- Basic warranty, to meet legal requirements

- Price, within 15 percent premium

- Awareness of XYZ as a supplier of forklifts

- Equipment delivery within one month of order

|  | Customers' qualifying needs: value screening equation | Customers' determining needs: value decision equation |
|---|---|---|
| Company strength: value advantage |  | (2) Leverage for differential value advantage |
| Competitive parity |  | (3) Enhance to achieve value advantage |
| Company weakness: value disadvantage | (1) Critical to qualify for consideration | (4) Improve If related need is important |

**Figure 7.6** Value opportunity identification matrix.

- Forklifts trucks must not tip easily

- Adequate aisle clearance

The planning team concluded that its major weakness regarding qualifiers pertained to the awareness issue, with only about 60 percent to 70 percent awareness that XYZ handled forklifts. Additionally, the team felt that they were unable to meet the delivery window approximately 5 percent of the time, and that there were, perhaps, 10 percent of local warehousing operations with aisles too narrow for their trucks.

With this information in hand, the forklift planning team was in a position to systematically identify its value-adding opportunities. In priority order, those were:

1. *Improve awareness and coverage (Q).*

2. *Expand the product line to include narrow-aisle machines (Q).*

3. *Improve the timeliness of equipment delivery (Q).*

4. *Improve to leverage XYZ's dealer service by focusing on:*
   a. *The ability to complete repair work (shop and field/warranty and nonwarranty) quickly and when promised*
   b. *The diagnostics skills of our service people (shop and field)*
   c. *The technical knowledge of our service technicians*
   d. *Quicker turnaround on major repairs*

5. *Improve to leverage (XYZ brand's) strong and recognized machine quality and brand image by emphasizing key features:*
   a. *Stability of machine*
   b. *Lifting capacity for size of machine*
   c. *Responsiveness of controls*
   d. *Machine durability and reliability that shows up in the amount of unscheduled downtime*

6. *Improve to leverage XYZ's dealer partnering by focusing on:*
   a. *Its high-quality sales personnel to provide reps who:*
      i. *Understand the needs of this segment's business*
      ii. *Demonstrate a high level of product knowledge*
      iii. *Have experience in equipment operation*
      iv. *Demonstrate the honesty of the dealership*
      v. *Show a solid understanding of the needs of the warehousing market*

7. *Improve to leverage XYZ's parts availability by focusing on:*
   a. *The ability to get parts to the customer quickly*
   b. *A sufficient stock of routine parts on hand*
   c. *Helping customers to determine their parts requirements*
   d. *Keeping customers informed of parts backorders*

8. *Improve to leverage price satisfaction*

**Table 7.2**   Head-to-head VPC analysis.

| | Lift Truck supplier | | | | | |
| --- | --- | --- | --- | --- | --- | --- |
| | Company XYZ | Competitor 1 | Competitor 2 | Competitor 3 | Competitor 4 | Competitor 5 |
| Ability to complete shop service work when promised | 7.54 | 6.44 | 6.57 | 8.13 | 7.13 | 7.40 |
| Dealer minimizes major repair turnaround time | 7.51 | 6.29 | 6.75 | 8.23 | 6.79 | 7.52 |
| Ability to diagnose machine problems | 7.61 | 7.63 | 7.27 | 8.56 | 7.40 | 7.38 |
| Diagnostic skills of field service people | 7.47 | 7.77 | 6.71 | 8.38 | 7.38 | 7.41 |
| Knowledge of service technicians | 7.80 | 7.64 | 7.53 | 8.62 | 7.19 | 8.22 |
| Providing quick field service | 8.09 | 6.18 | 6.64 | 8.15 | 6.14 | 6.32 |

| | XYZ advantage | | XYZ parity | | XYZ disadvantage |
| --- | --- | --- | --- | --- | --- |

The detail listed under each opportunity is derived through an examination of XYZ's comparative performance on the attributes (VPCS) comprising each quality driver, an example of which is shown in Table 7.2.

Based on information from the competitive value matrix (Figure 7.4), XYZ's desired strategic position is to become the undisputed value leader, differentiating itself from the rest of the competition by moving toward the upper right-hand corner of the matrix. XYZ's business objective is to achieve improved ratings on both the quality and price drivers of value, but it plans to do that while also increasing profits. This means that XYZ surely doesn't want to lower prices, and will probably need to include some actions to reduce costs as well. In order to determine how this might be done, the forklift planning team turned to a Market Value Simulator$^{sm}$ to test a variety of different scenarios. Figure 7.7 shows XYZ's current value model ratings and the resulting competitive landscape.

Because CQI and price are highly correlated ($r = .83$), the forklift planning team knew that any increases in quality perceptions would be accompanied by increases in price perceptions. Similarly, because quality and image are also intercorrelated ($r = .66$), increases in quality performance would also result in an image improvement. Therefore, improved performance on the quality drivers would produce the desired results for price satisfaction and image as well. After running several "what-if" scenarios, the

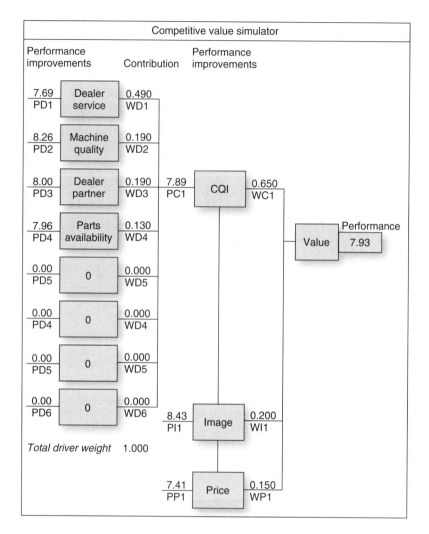

**Figure 7.7a** Simulation at $T_1$.

quality driver improvements shown in Figure 7.8 produced the desired results vis-à-vis value differentiation.

This scenario required the most substantial performance improvement on the number-one quality driver, dealer service. This is also the driver that is most directly under the control of the dealer. Although the planning team knew they would not have much direct influence on improvements in machine quality, ratings on the machine quality attributes suggested some perceptual issues that might be addressed through better communications. Most importantly, if XYZ could achieve the identified quality performance im-

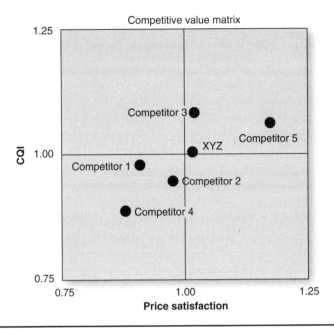

**Figure 7.7b**   Simulation at $T_1$.

provements, both price and image ratings would improve as well. And, improvements in XYZ's ratings would impact the overall market averages on quality and price, thereby effectively driving XYZ's competitors to the lower-left quadrant of the matrix.

Recall, too, that XYZ's business objectives placed special emphasis on customer retention. Therefore, the competitive strategy for this product/market must emphasize performance on those drivers most relevant to customer loyalty. Figure 7.9 illustrates the distribution of XYZ's current customer base. Note that 35 percent of XYZ's customers already view their relationship with XYZ as one of outstanding value. Another 33 percent are in the "outstanding value" quadrant, but are at somewhat greater risk. And 24 percent are on the verge of defecting for a better value offering. The 8 percent in Group 4 may already be unreachable. Clearly, XYZ needs to focus on customers in Groups 2 and 3. Table 7.3 provides insight into vulnerabilities among these two groups. The scores in the table are based on average performance scores where 1 = poor performance and 10 = superior performance. In both of the targeted groups, XYZ's greatest vulnerability is on the dealer service driver. An emphasis on this driver in the competitive strategy will therefore serve the purpose of placing the appropriate focus on customer retention.

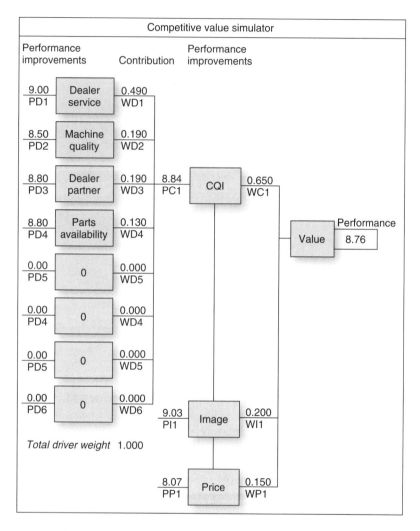

**Figure 7.8a** Simulation at $T_4$.

Based on this information, the forklift planning team articulated the following strategy:

### Product/Market Strategy

*To become the undisputed value leader by:*

- *Improving awareness of our product offering and associated services, and improving sales coverage*

- *Improving to leverage our dealer service*

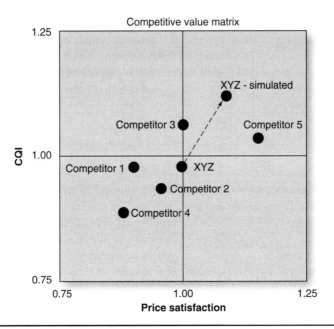

**Figure 7.8b**  Simulation at $T_4$.

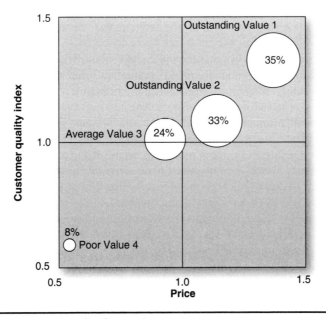

**Figure 7.9**  Customer loyalty matrix.

95

**Table 7.3** Value group driver ratings.

|  | Outstanding Value 1 | Outstanding Value 2 | Average Value 3 | Poor Value 4 |
|---|---|---|---|---|
| Dealer service | 9.30 | (6.96) | (6.77) | 3.94 |
| Machine quality | 9.59 | 8.04 | 7.26 | 3.60 |
| Dealer partner | 9.29 | 7.72 | 7.40 | 4.44 |
| Parts availability | 9.44 | 7.96 | 6.88 | 4.25 |

- *Improving to leverage [XYZ brand's] strong and recognized machine quality and brand image by emphasizing key features*

- *Improving to leverage our partnering capabilities by focusing on our high-quality sales personnel*

- *Improving to leverage our parts supply*

The first opportunity listed in the strategy pertains to a qualifier and must be addressed if the organization is going to be considered as a competitive alternative by the entire market. The remaining three opportunities correspond to the drivers on which the organization is at parity with its targeted competitor. Notice that not all value opportunities identified earlier are included in the strategy. The strategy focuses on those opportunities that provide the greatest chance for achieving the organization's product/market objectives. Clearly, the earlier list is too lengthy and complex, violating one of the important rules of strategy formulation—keep it simple.

A check on the efficacy of the strategy is to ask a simple question: "If the organization executes on each of the opportunities listed in the strategy statement, will it accomplish its product/market objectives?" No one, of course, will know with any certainty. However, if it is obvious that they will not, other opportunities generated from their strengths and weaknesses can be identified.

In order for this strategy to be effective it must be communicated to the entire organization. Too often strategies are top secret, with few in the organization aware of what the company is really trying to accomplish. One CEO insisted that every one of his managers knew and understood the company's strategy. In a subsequent meeting all managers were asked to write down, on a piece of paper, what the organization's strategy was. Of the 10 managers present, 5 wrote a $ sign, 3 wrote a "?", and 2 wrote nothing. A strategy must be communicated and understood, both internally and externally, if it is to be effective. This is yet another reason for keeping the strategy simple.

A strategy should communicate precisely what the target is (undisputed value leader), and generally and simply, how the organization will work to attain that target (improving to leverage four opportunities). To identify and choose an *intended or desired organizational* value proposition requires answering the following questions:

- What are your product/market business objectives?

- What assumptions underlie these objectives?

- What competitive strategy will lead to the attainment of those objectives?

- Which of your existing market opportunities should become part of that strategy?

Effective management of the organization's value proposition to move from its current state to its desired state will involve application of the marketing mix to each of the strategic opportunities, along with action steps and the budget necessary to fully capitalize on each opportunity. That application is the subject of the next Chapter.

# 8

# How Does the Organization Manage Its Value Proposition?

The development of a competitive market strategy, described in the previous Chapter, is both systematic and straightforward. Linking value-based market needs with the organization's competitive strengths and weaknesses ensures that the strategy will be market driven and that it will maximize the return on any investment required because of the emphasis on leveraging competitive strengths. But the effectiveness of any strategy is only as good as the steps taken to deploy that strategy. And that requires setting clear objectives regarding elements of the marketing mix, detailing the actions necessary to attain those objectives, and specifying the costs of those action programs so that a comparison of projected costs with forecasted revenues will enable management to assess the viability of the plan prior to implementation.

## MARKETING MIX OBJECTIVES

In contrast with the exogenous variables monitored through systematic environmental scanning (see Appendix B), the four elements of the marketing mix—product, price, promotion, and place (distribution)—are directly under your organization's control. Effective and efficient competition requires the correct assemblage of these elements to execute the strategy and achieve the product/market objectives.

The competitive strategy for a product/market consists of a specified set of market opportunities driven by market perspectives on value. A unique marketing mix must be applied to each opportunity in order to fully capitalize on that opportunity. To illustrate, we'll continue the forklift/warehousing example developed in the previous Chapter. The forklift planning team articulated their strategy as follows:

### Product/Market Strategy

*To become the undisputed value leader by:*

- *Improving awareness of our product offering and associated services, and improving sales coverage*

- *Improving to leverage our dealer service*

- *Improving to leverage [XYZ brand's] strong and recognized machine quality and brand image by emphasizing key features*

- *Improving to leverage our partnering capabilities by focusing on our high-quality sales personnel*

- *Improving to leverage our parts supply*

This competitive strategy is comprised of five of the previously identified eight opportunities, one to address a qualifier based on awareness, and four to address the quality drivers from the value model. Of the four marketing mix elements, some will be more appropriate to a specific opportunity than others. For example, the first opportunity pertaining to awareness can be addressed exclusively through the "promotion" element of the mix. No product, distribution, or pricing objectives are necessary in order to fully capitalize on this opportunity. The second opportunity, however, will clearly require specific objectives pertaining to product (dealer service) and promotion, because any improvements in service will need to be communicated as well. There may even be distribution objectives required to capitalize on this opportunity, depending upon locational issues associated with providing timely service. The complete list of marketing mix objectives, as determined by the forklift planning team, is provided in Figure 8.1.

Each objective is stated in terms of the intended outcome. This precise identification of the intended target provides a high degree of measurability. For example, Opportunity 2, objective 2.3 is very precise: "**95%** of all breakdown problems **correctly diagnosed** in the field **within 2 hours** of arrival on site." There is no doubt regarding the specificity of the objective and what is actually expected. Contrast this with the usual wording of this type of objective: "Improve diagnostic skills." How does the organization know how much improvement is necessary? Is just a marginal improvement a sign of accomplishing the objective? Clearly, the former is more specific and provides significantly greater guidance than the latter. This is where many organizations stumble in the development of their plans. The lack of specificity in the declaration of objectives impedes the need for actionability.

Each opportunity requires a different marketing mix. Some will only require an effective communications program to increase awareness, as in Opportunity 1. Some will require changes in the product as delivered,

**Opportunity 1: Improving awareness of our product and associated services, and improving sales coverage:**

Promotion:

1.1 Attain 70% unaided awareness of XYZ as a supplier of forklifts by end of 2006

1.2 Attain 85% unaided awareness of XYZ as a supplier of forklifts by end of 2007

1.3 Attain 95% unaided awareness of XYZ as a supplier of forklifts by end of 2008

1.4 50% of all warehousing customers likely to buy 1 or more forklifts within 1 year will receive a face-to-face sales call once/quarter

1.5 XYZ in on 55% of all forklift deals by end of 2008

**Opportunity 2: Improve to leverage XYZ's dealer service**

Product

2.1 95% of all shop and field service work completed on time as promised

2.2 Major repair (e.g., drive train) completion times reduced by 25% from current levels

2.3 95% of all breakdown problems correctly diagnosed in the field within 2 hours of arrival on site (same criterion in shop for equipment delivered by customer)

Place/Distribution

2.4 All emergency breakdowns (metro areas) responded to on-site within 2 hours

2.5 80% on-site response of 4 – 6 hours in non-metro areas (within 75 miles of branch)

Promotion/Communication

2.6 For every repair situation (outside field), customer notified of repair status every 24 hours

**Opportunity 3: Improve to leverage [Brand Name]'s strong and recognized machine quality and brand image by emphasizing key features**

Product:

3.1 All new machine deliveries accompanied by DVD on safe and effective operation

3.2 All machine deliveries to customers who have not previously owned a [Brand Name] forklift accompanied by 1-hour live operations demonstration

Following are features that should be demonstrably superior:

Larger drive motors compared to all other competitors

Speed

Turning radius

Smooth braking

Promotion

3.3 50% of FL/Warehousing market rate [Brand Name] forklifts as providing superior operator comfort, durability, ease of on/off, and ease of operation relative to [Competitor 3] and all other major players

3.4 50% of FL/Warehousing market rate [Brand Name] accessibility of work areas for scheduled servicing as being superior

**Opportunity 4: Improve to leverage XYZ's dealer partnering by focusing on our high-quality sales personnel**

*Continued*

**Figure 8.1** Marketing mix objectives.

*Continued*

"Product"

4.1 All sales reps capable of operating a forklift to level 1 of operator competency

4.2 Sales reps capable of explaining functionality of every aspect of [Brand Name] and key competitive forklifts

4.3 Sales reps demonstrate working knowledge of accounting, tax, depreciation, financial operations of the client's business pertinent to warehousing customers

4.4 All warehousing reps understand current and prospective projects in the region

Promotion

4.5 All warehousing reps understand and able to deliver the company's core values (pertains to ethics, integrity, honesty, excellence in all things)

4.6 80% of warehousing market aware of XYZ commitment to warehousing market with [location] facility and dedicated personnel

**Opportunity 5: Improve to leverage XYZ dealer parts supply**

Product/Place

5.1 Normal wear and service parts available to all warehousing customers w/in 2 hours
  • "A" warehouses have 72-hour supply of both wear parts and routine maintenance parts on site, on consignment
  • "B" warehouses have 72-hour supply of routine maintenance parts on site, on consignment; wear parts delivered w/in 8 hours
  • "C" warehouses receive all parts orders w/in 24 hours

5.2 No mechanical repair delayed more than 24 hours due to lack of parts

Promotion/Communication

5.3 50% of the market rates XYZ as the most convenient, reliable, and responsive supplier of forklift parts by EOY 2006

5.4 60% of the market rates XYZ as the most convenient, reliable, and responsive supplier of forklift parts by EOY 2007

5.5 70% of the market rates XYZ as the most convenient, reliable, and responsive supplier of forklift parts by EOY 2008

5.6 All warehousing customers notified within 2 hours of change to status of parts backorder

**Other**

Other 1 95% of customers on the warehousing list validated as owning multiple forklifts and working primarily in warehousing-type applications

Other 2 Develop process to enable tracking of parts and service by product/market

**Figure 8.1**  Marketing mix objectives.

along with more focused communications to address perceptual issues in the marketplace. This is certainly the case with regard to Opportunity 3. Note that none of these opportunities require specific objectives pertaining to price, although the planning team might have made explicit the fact that they intend to pass along the 3 percent cost increase identified earlier as an assumption.

Many plans require the explicit articulation of objectives that don't fit neatly within one of the marketing mix elements. In this case, the team identified two "other" objectives, one pertaining to cleaning up the data in the CRM system and the other pertaining to more definitive tracking of information within the business information system.

Market value opportunities are general in nature and require the explication of specific objectives in order to make clear the intended targets. The next step is to identify the action programs necessary to achieve the objectives.

# PRODUCT/MARKET ACTION PROGRAMS

Actions convert the objectives into concrete results. They provide the stepping stone for plan deployment and, as such, are an extremely important part of the competitive planning process. One set of actions from the forklift/warehousing plan is presented in Table 8.1. This action program follows from market value Opportunity 2, the opportunity to improve and leverage dealer service. In this case the action steps articulate the deployment of a Six Sigma project designed to enhance and leverage dealer service, in particular the timeliness of equipment repairs. Action steps, in general, provide the linkage between the organization's strategy and Six Sigma initiatives, a topic to be discussed and illustrated in the next Chapter.

All actions must be accompanied by "key milestones" that indicate when the action is to be completed. This provides a check so that the planning team can make sure the plan deployment is on schedule and, if not, why not.

In addition, each action has a "performance measure" that indicates how the team knows the action has been completed. It is not sufficient to simply state that the action is done. For example, if an action requires that customers be made aware of their local dealer, it is not sufficient to simply run an ad awareness campaign. Instead it will require a survey to test for the awareness level. That requires measurement, which, again, is another area in which many plans fail.

Responsibilities must also be assigned. Actions need not be carried out by an actual planning team member but there must be a team member who is responsible for seeing that the action is, indeed, carried out. Too often plan implementation fails because individuals let actions fall between the cracks. "I thought you were taking care of that" and the reply "Well, I thought you were taking care of that" are often heard. The result is that nothing gets done. Assigning responsibilities goes a long way to cementing up the cracks and moving the plan forward.

Finally, there is usually, but not always, a direct cost associated with the accomplishment of an action. This should be posted. The example in Table 8.1 shows no direct costs for this set of actions. Company XYZ has

**Table 8.1** Product/market action program—service.

**Objective 2.1: 95% of service work to be completed on time as promised**

| Actions | Key milestone | Performance measures | Responsibility | Cost |
|---|---|---|---|---|
| Assess performance gaps on CTQ factors relative to Competitor 3 | April 2005 | Performance gaps quantified and rank-ordered based on their importance | John Schimmel | -0- |
| Identify performance gaps relative to Competitor 3 for each performance attribute within the most important CTQ factor | April 2005 | Importance weights established for each performance attribute | John Schimmel | -0- |
| Flesh out Y Platform to confirm value stream for analysis | May 2005 | $Y$ = #1 CTQ; Sub-$Y$'s = Performance attributes with importance weights. Identification of input processes ($X$'s) affecting the outputs ($Y$'s) | Jim Plummer | -0- |
| Develop and evaluate CTQ/process matrix | May 2005 | Impact of processes on attributes assessed and weights assigned. Processes ranked in terms of impact on quality driver attributes and cost. | Jim Plummer | -0- |
| Develop map of value stream | May 2005 | Skeletal map of complete value stream with swim lanes. Detailed map of priority processes. Problem areas identified. | Roger Lauck | -0- |
| Select/define Lean Six Sigma projects | June 2005 | Impact of identified problems on quality driver and on cost assessed. Opportunities and objectives identified. Rank order based on impact. Top 3 opportunities selected. Approval by Lean Six Sigma Sponsor | Peter Hall | -0- |
| Determine baseline performance criteria | July 2005 | % of work orders with promise dates included. % of completes within promise date. % defects, etc. | John Schimmel | -0- |

determined to identify and include only incremental costs in the plan, not costs that simply represent a reallocation of personnel time. The totality of the direct incremental costs will be later collected for the "plan cost," which is necessary for determining the plan contribution.

The action plan for objective 2.1 is detailed only to the point where Six Sigma projects are identified. Subsequent action steps will be dependent on that determination, and are added to the plan at the appropriate time. This makes the plan a "living plan," not one that is developed at a single point in time, then dusted off in a year for review.

The action program for objective 4.2 is shown in Table 8.2. This action program addresses the substantive changes in training required to provide an effective communications program through the organization's sales force. This is a partial listing of actions for another of XYZ's objectives. The actions begin with an assessment of the sales reps' skill levels. This is necessary in order to understand the level at which sales reps can perform the desired tasks. Depending on the results of this assessment, some reps may require further training, while others may not. The action program also calls for an annual assessment by the specified milestone. This points out the "living nature" of the competitive plan. In this case, training programs are not rigidly applied for all reps but the annual performance assessment ensures that high skill levels are maintained.

# BUDGETS AND FORECASTS

Once actions have been developed for each of the objectives, it is now possible to add up the incremental direct costs and assign them to various categories. A form for doing this is shown in Figure 8.2.

The individual expense categories are arbitrary and are shown for illustrative purposes only. The categories should be tailored to meet the needs of the individual organization. Costs can be posted from previous quarters to show changes over time. Costs can also be estimated for any number of out years that are relevant to the organization.

Many organizations find that their accounting systems are initially unable to allocate costs by product/market, and there are some costs that should probably never be allocated on that basis. The point is that most organizations initially deal with both costs and revenues on an incremental basis. We've already noted that costs on the action programs form are incremental costs only. Therefore, costs in the "cost category" part of the budget form should also be restricted to incremental costs. That said, developing a budget this way will also cause the accounting division to begin tracking costs and revenues on a product/market basis. In turn, this will ensure that future analyses of the product/market matrix are more factual.

**Table 8.2** Product/market action program—sales.

| Actions | Key milestone | Performance measures | Responsibility | Cost |
|---|---|---|---|---|
| Identify skills base of all sales & PRS reps on [XYZ's OEM] and competitive lift trucks. | July 2005 | Individual performance scores for reps on skills matrix. Deficiencies identified. | Paul Finch | $0 |
| Develop training program with [OEM] and XYZ. | Sept. 2005 | Training modules for deficiencies identified. | Paul Finch | $0 |
| Purchase [OEM] and competitive parts for comparison display and training needs. | Sept. 2005 | Key wear parts acquired and evaluated for durability. | Tom Pinkert | $10,000 |
| Investigate the purchase/loan/ of key competitive forklifts [Competitors 1, 2, and 3]. | Dec. 2005 | Feasibility assessment of attaining equip. | Tom Pinkert | $120,000 |
| Carry out Theoretical and In the Iron Training for all reps. | Feb. 2006 | Each rep must be able to competently conduct an "in iron presentation." | Paul Finch | $5,000 |
| Carry out annual review of reps' competency on XYZ and competitive machines. | Feb. Annually | Individual performance scores for reps on skills matrix. | Paul Finch | $0 |
| Train reps as needed as per action 5. | March/April Annually | As per objective. | Paul Finch | $0 |

Product/market _____     Date: _____

| Cost category | Last year | This year | | | | Year 1 | Year 2 | Year 3 | Year 4 | Year 5 |
|---|---|---|---|---|---|---|---|---|---|---|
| | | Q1 | Q2 | Q3 | Q4 | | | | | |
| Sales expense | | | | | | | | | | |
| Service expense | | | | | | | | | | |
| Marketing expense | | | | | | | | | | |
| Other direct expense | | | | | | | | | | |
| Total expense | | | | | | | | | | |

| Contributions | Last year | This year | | | | Year 1 | Year 2 | Year 3 | Year 4 | Year 5 |
|---|---|---|---|---|---|---|---|---|---|---|
| | | Q1 | Q2 | Q3 | Q4 | | | | | |
| Plan revenue | | | | | | | | | | |
| Plan contribution | | | | | | | | | | |

**Figure 8.2**   Budget and market forecast.

Plan revenue is estimated by translating product/market objectives regarding market share into revenues. Care must be taken to account for market growth rates, typically identified explicitly in the "assumptions" section of the plan. Also, incremental revenues should not include the cost of goods sold. Again, depending on the focus of the plan, these revenues can be estimated for any number of out years. Subtracting the estimated direct costs from the estimated plan revenues provides the estimated plan contribution, or how much marginal revenue is expected by the deployment of the plan. In some cases, plan contribution may be negative in the early deployment periods. If the plan is efficacious, these negative revenues should turn positive in succeeding time periods.

One final note: There will be instances when the plan contribution appears to be surprisingly small. One explanation may be that the planning team has neglected to include revenue that may seem ancillary to the plan. For example, with a focus on forklifts to the warehousing market, the team may fail to include the incremental parts and service revenue that accrues from having a larger machine population at work in their service area. Moreover, there may be a significant spillover into other product/markets as a result of the discipline introduced by this competitive market planning process. For example, one financial services firm focused on mortgages for the "full-nest I" market and discovered that the disciplined focus on that market segment resulted in substantial increases in checking and savings activity from that same segment. A supplier of farm equipment focused on mid-sized tractors for dairy farmers and subsequently noted substantial sales increases in other farm equipment to that market segment as well. And, as has been reported by companies that embark on a Six Sigma journey, companies that embrace this disciplined approach to competitive planning frequently find that the very culture change produced by the approach results in higher productivity throughout the organization.

# 9

# The Value-Strategy-
# Process Linkage

Achieving superior market performance means doing things differently, especially if your organization is not the value leader. Doing the same thing over and over and expecting different results is not only silly, it is wasteful, both economically and strategically. Yet this is the exact behavior many organizations embrace. If your organization is facing a value disadvantage, it is the current policies and strategies of the organization that have produced or fostered the disadvantage. In the words of Albert Einstein:

*You can't solve current problems with current thinking. Current problems are the result of current thinking.*

Current policies and practices are not likely to close a value gap between your organization and a value leader. Likewise, if your organization enjoys a value advantage, increasing that advantage and widening the value gap will require constant attention to those processes identified within your product/market strategies as critical to quality performance.

There is a well-defined process for linking the value-based voice of the customer to the key processes for Six Sigma or lean initiatives. This process is shown in Figure 9.1. The process begins with understanding how specific targeted customers using specific product lines define value, and how they perceive the value propositions of competing suppliers. The basis for acquiring that understanding was described in Chapters 3 through 6, and includes modeling value, highlighting competitive strengths and weaknesses on key quality drivers, and identifying existing market-based opportunities for value enhancements.

The process of linking value to strategy begins with carefully articulating key business performance objectives, such as revenue, profitability, and market share goals. This is followed by targeting the value proposition

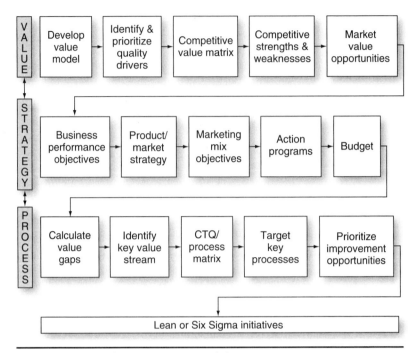

**Figure 9.1**   The value-strategy-process linkage.

that will enable the organization to achieve those objectives, then identifying the market value opportunities to incorporate in the strategy in order to achieve the desired value proposition. Chapters 7 and 8 described how to complete that process, fleshing out the competitive marketing strategy with marketing mix objectives, action programs, and supporting budgets.

Many of those strategic objectives and actions require substantial changes in the organization's business processes. And, while most business managers would publicly endorse the need to constantly monitor and improve their business processes, the challenge lies in making the linkage from the voice of the customer through the strategy to the process improvement initiatives so explicit that everyone in the organization understands precisely what is driving those process improvements (the customer) and any associated cost reductions (only those non-value-adding costs).

This Chapter picks up the discussion by illustrating how to calculate competitive gaps in quality drivers—the differences between your organization and a targeted competitor. That calculation will direct the organization's attention to those value streams most critical to superior value creation and delivery. Having identified the quality driver that is the most critical-to-quality factor (CTQ, in Six Sigma parlance), the next step is to link the CTQ to processes within the value stream for detailed process mapping, then to rank order impediments to value creation and delivery in order to identify key opportunities for process improvement initiatives. These are the lean and Six Sigma projects that are now ensured of having strategic implications because they are being directed by market perspectives on value.

At this point in the process, the critical-to-quality factors have been identified and prioritized. The organization understands what its competitive value proposition is and what it must focus on to improve or enhance its value offering. It understands what kind of value gap, whether positive or negative, it faces. Your organization will choose to be a value *leader* (seeking to widen its value advantage over a targeted competitor), a *challenger* (seeking to lessen the value advantage between your organization and a targeted competitor), or a *follower* (maintain the value difference without losing ground between your organization and a targeted competitor). Whatever the strategic decision, the linkage from value to strategy is complete. The next step is to ensure an explicit linkage to process improvements.

# CALCULATE CRITICAL VALUE GAPS

There are two levels at which value gaps exist—at the quality-driver level (CTQ factors) and at the value-performance-criteria level. The value gaps at each level provide the basis for identifying which value streams and which processes within those value streams should become the focus for specific process improvement initiatives.

The mechanics of identifying the value gaps at the CTQ level are shown in Table 9.1. For the purpose of continuity, we'll continue with the forklift/warehousing planning example. Recall that there were four quality drivers in this product/market, that no competitor had a differential value advantage, and that Company XYZ had elected to target Competitor 3 to become the undisputed value leader.

The quality drivers from the value model, or critical-to-quality factors in Six Sigma parlance, are shown in the left-hand column. The importance of each quality driver, also extracted directly from the value model, is shown in the second column. Mean scores on the CTQ's for Company XYZ and each

**Table 9.1**  Calculation of CTQ gaps.

| CTQ Factor | Importance | XYZ | Competitor 1 | Competitor 2 | Competitor 3 | Competitor 4 | Competitor 5 | Value gap (XYZ – 3) | Gap importance |
|---|---|---|---|---|---|---|---|---|---|
| Dealer service | 0.49 | 7.69 | 7.20 | 7.01 | 8.35 | 6.93 | 7.41 | −0.66 | −0.32 |
| Machine quality | 0.19 | 8.26 | 8.27 | 8.32 | 8.48 | 7.84 | 9.09 | −0.22 | −0.04 |
| Dealer partner | 0.19 | 8.00 | 7.38 | 6.97 | 8.19 | 7.14 | 8.05 | −0.19 | −0.04 |
| Parts availability | 0.13 | 7.96 | 6.47 | 6.97 | 7.70 | 6.82 | 8.32 | 0.26 | 0.03 |

competitor are provided again in the next six columns. The column headed "Value gap" indicates the difference in scores between XYZ and Competitor 3, the targeted competitor of focus in this situation. Notice, too, that the value gaps are all negative, consistent with the value positioning of the two competitors in Figure 7.4. "Gap importance" (last column) is the product of the value gap times the importance of the CTQ factor. In this case, the number-one CTQ factor (dealer service) has the highest absolute gap importance score (.32). The number-one CTQ factor will not always produce the highest gap importance score. Gap importance is a function not only of the importance of the CTQ factor but also the magnitude of the gap between the two competitors. The remaining quality drivers are much less important in terms of closing the value gap and moving into value leadership, both because dealer service is the most important quality driver (0.49) and because the gap in performance between XYZ and Competitor 3 is largest on that CTQ (−0.66).

## IDENTIFY THE KEY VALUE STREAM

Though many treat value streams and processes as identical, we believe there is a fundamental distinguishing difference between the two. We define a value stream as the comprehensive set of activities and communications that collectively creates and delivers value to the customer, or end user. A value stream begins with a customer's need for a product or service and ends with that customer's belief that he or she has received something of genuine value, as illustrated in Figure 9.2.

Value streams are typically made up of several interconnected processes and involve any number of functional areas within the organization. The key distinction between a value stream and the numerous organizational processes that comprise it is that the value stream exists to deliver value to

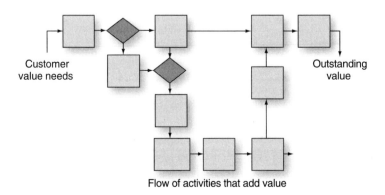

Customer value needs

Outstanding value

Flow of activities that add value

**Figure 9.2** Customer-focused value stream.

an *external* customer, the one whose perception of value delivery will keep the organization profitable.

The process of delivering parts to a service bay (internal customer) within an automobile dealership is a good example of a process that may be part of a value stream but which is not a value stream in and of itself. Similarly, accounting systems (within a manufacturing organization) include a variety of processes such as invoicing, tracking of accounts receivable and accounts payable, posting of monthly profit and loss statements, and so on. These processes may be very important to any number of internal customers, but will not necessarily constitute a value stream, which has as its focus the external customer. Value streams typically include processes that are relevant to both internal and external customers, but the complete value stream begins and ends with the external customer, who is the ultimate arbiter of value.

In the current situation, the forklift distributor has three basic value streams: an order-to-delivery value stream for customer acquisition of new and used Forklifts, a parts distribution value stream for customers who do their own repairs or who keep maintenance parts at their local warehouse, and a service/repair value stream for customers who need equipment serviced by a third party. Within each of these general value streams, there may be subcategories. For example, the specific processes included within the order-to-delivery of new forklifts may be somewhat different from the specific processes associated with used equipment purchases. Similarly, the repair of a major component on a forklift would likely entail a different set of processes than would a minor repair completed on site.

The calculation of CTQ value gaps and the emergence of dealer service as the critical CTQ factor, shown in Table 9.1, make it clear that the general value stream for further focus should be the service/repair value stream. But what aspects of the service/repair value stream need focus—all of it, or only a part? In order to get more specific about a subcategory, the planning team conducted a second-order analysis of CTQ gaps, focusing this time on the individual performance criteria within the CTQ of dealer service. The result of that analysis is shown in Table 9.2.

The first column of the matrix in Table 9.2 identifies the CTQ factor, in this case dealer service. The next column shows the weights of the individual value performance criteria (VPC). These weights can be calculated in one of two ways. In the present case, the correlation between the individual value performance criterion and the driver, or CTQ factor, is used. This provides an indication of how important each VPC is to the driver or CTQ factor. A second manner of calculating importance is to use the factor loadings of the individual value performance criteria. This provides a similar measure of importance. (For a more thorough discussion of factors and factor loadings, see Reidenbach et al., *Dominating Markets with Value: Advances in Customer Value Management,* Rhumb Line Publishing, 2000, Chapter 5). The two approaches will give proximate similarity in rankings, but will not be identical.

**Table 9.2**    Value performance criteria gaps.

| CTQ factor | VPC importance | Value performance criteria | XYZ | Competitor 1 | Competitor 2 | Competitor 3 | Competitor 4 | Competitor 5 | Value gap (XYZ − 3) | Importance |
|---|---|---|---|---|---|---|---|---|---|---|
| Dealer service | 0.85 | Ability to complete shop service when promised | 7.54 | 6.44 | 6.57 | 8.13 | 7.13 | 7.40 | −0.59 | −0.50 |
| | 0.81 | Dealer minimizes major repair turnaround time | 7.51 | 6.29 | 6.75 | 8.23 | 6.79 | 7.52 | −0.72 | −0.58 |
| | 0.78 | Ability to diagnose machine problems | 7.61 | 7.63 | 7.27 | 8.56 | 7.40 | 7.38 | −0.95 | −0.74 |
| | 0.72 | Diagnostic skills of field service people | 7.47 | 7.77 | 6.71 | 8.38 | 7.38 | 7.41 | −0.91 | −0.66 |
| | 0.63 | Knowledge of service technicians | 7.80 | 7.64 | 7.63 | 8.62 | 7.19 | 8.22 | −0.82 | −0.52 |
| | 0.60 | Providing quality field service/ quick field service | 8.09 | 6.18 | 6.64 | 8.15 | 6.14 | 6.32 | −0.06 | −0.04 |

The value performance criteria are listed in the third column with mean scores for the XYZ and its five competitors listed in the next six columns. The mechanics for calculating the importance of the individual value performance criteria are the same as discussed earlier for the CTQs in Table 9.1. The value gaps between XYZ and Competitor 3 for each value performance criterion are calculated and then multiplied by the VPC attribute weight to obtain the importance scores shown in the last column.

The value gap importance shown in the last column indicates the relative importance of each value performance criterion in either widening or closing the value gap between XYZ and Competitor 3.

The dealer service CTQ factor and the individual value performance criteria point to major component repairs as being the value stream most important for enhancing value. For example, value performance criteria such as

- Ability to complete shop service when promised

- Dealer minimizes major repair turnaround time

- Ability to diagnose machine problems

- Diagnostic skills of field service people

clearly indicate that the type of service to be addressed pertains to major component repairs, such as a drive train failure, as opposed to more routine repairs.

Once the key value stream has been identified it is necessary to decompose the value stream into its constituent processes. In this case, the service/repair value stream is comprised of the following processes:

- Repair inquiry process

- Scheduling process

- Inspection/diagnostic process

- Repair process

- Parts supply to workshop process

- Transport process

- Warranty process

- Credit checking process

- Parts crediting process

- Invoicing process

In continuing toward the degree of focus required in order to identify value-enhancing opportunities for targeted process improvements, it is necessary to determine which processes within the value stream are currently having the greatest impact on the organization's ability to create and deliver value. For that determination, we turn to a CTQ/process matrix analysis.

## CONSTRUCTING THE CTQ/PROCESS MATRIX

Once the value stream and its component processes have been identified the next step is to identify the most important processes that will become the fo-

**Table 9.3** CTQ/process matrix.

| | Ability to complete shop service when promised | Dealer minimizes major repair turnaround time | Ability to diagnose machine problems | Diagnostic skills of field service people | Knowledge of service technicians | Provision of quality field service/quick field service | Process importance |
|---|---|---|---|---|---|---|---|
| **VPC importance** | 0.50 | 0.58 | 0.74 | 0.66 | 0.52 | 0.04 | |
| **Repair VS processes** | | | | | | | |
| **Inquiry** | 6 | 3 | 0 | 0 | 6 | 3 | 7.98 |
| **Scheduling** | 9 | 6 | 3 | 0 | 3 | 3 | 11.88 |
| **Inspection** | 6 | 6 | 9 | 9 | 9 | 3 | 23.88 |
| **Repair** | 9 | 9 | 9 | 9 | 9 | 9 | 27.36 |
| **Parts supply** | 9 | 9 | 3 | 3 | 0 | 3 | 14.04 |
| **Transport** | 6 | 3 | 0 | 0 | 3 | 3 | 6.42 |
| **Warranty** | 0 | 3 | 3 | 3 | 3 | 0 | 7.50 |
| **Credit checking** | 3 | 0 | 0 | 0 | 0 | 0 | 1.50 |
| **Parts crediting** | 3 | 0 | 0 | 0 | 3 | 0 | 3.06 |
| **Invoicing** | 0 | 0 | 0 | 0 | 3 | 0 | 1.56 |

cus of the organization's lean or Six Sigma efforts. Which of Company XYZ's processes should be targeted for Six Sigma initiatives? Table 9.3 shows how the value performance criteria coupled with the value gaps are used to pinpoint the crucial processes.

In Table 9.3, the service/repair value stream processes are arrayed down the left side of the matrix. Across the top are the value performance criteria that comprise the dealer service CTQ. Under each value performance criterion is the importance score derived from Table 9.2. This is the score that was calculated by multiplying the value performance criterion importance weight by the value gap/difference score (XYZ − Competitor 3).

Populating the main body of the matrix are evaluations of the impact that each individual process has on the performance scores of the individual criteria. These evaluations were made by a team of sales, service, and parts people, as well as a Six Sigma Black Belt from the XYZ organization. This multifunction approach captures a more global understanding of the impact individual processes have on the outputs than if a single person or functional area had completed the analysis. To a certain degree, these individual impact scores represent a "correlation" between the inputs (processes) and the outputs (value performance criteria).

The scoring process follows a relatively simple approach. A high impact is scored as a "9," a moderate impact a "6," a minimal impact a "3," and no impact a "0." For example, a score of 0 in the first row, third cell indicates that the team felt that the performance of the inquiry process had no impact on customer evaluations of the diagnostic skills of field service people. At the other end of the evaluative spectrum, a score of 9 in the "scheduling/ability to complete shop service work when promised" cell signifies that the team felt that the scheduling process had a strong impact on customer evaluations of the organization's ability to complete work when promised.

At the far right of the matrix is a column representing the summated products of the individual evaluations and the corresponding importance of the value performance criteria. The higher the score, the greater the impact the process has on the value performance criterion. Put another way, the higher the score the greater impact the input (process) has on the output (value performance criterion score). Because the objective is to identify the key processes that have the greatest impact on the dealer support CTQ, the scores identify the repair process, the inspection/diagnostics process, and the parts supply process as the most important. By focusing Six Sigma projects on these three processes, the dealer service CTQ will experience the greatest improvement.

## TARGET PROCESSES FOR SIX SIGMA OR LEAN PROJECTS

Should not all processes receive the attention of Six Sigma projects? No. First, this is too great an undertaking. It would take too much time and resources. Second, many of the processes do not contribute significantly to the gap issue facing the organization.

The methodology of using the voice of the customer eliminates agendas and opinions from the process and instead supplants them with facts. These facts come from the actual source of the definer of value, the customer.

Within our current example, XYZ has the greatest potential for breaking free from value parity with Competitor 3 by focusing on the repair process (27.36). Other candidate processes would include the inspection/diagnosis process (23.88) and the parts supply process (14.04). Company XYZ is in an enviable position here. Through analysis of the dealer service value stream as it pertains to major component repairs, XYZ's management may well identify opportunities to reduce the costs of value creation and delivery. More important, however, they may identify opportunities to decrease repair turnaround times and complete repairs by promise dates, which in turn would translate into real differential strategic advantages on a critical-to-quality driver. It doesn't take much imagination to see how the combination of such opportunities could lead to real and profitable increases in market share.

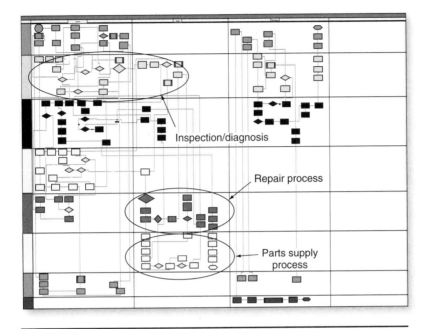

**Figure 9.3** The service/repair value stream map.

Once the value stream and processes have been identified, the mapping of the value stream, with specific attention to the key processes, can be done. It's important to note that the entire value stream must be mapped, albeit in skeletal form. If the value mapping is limited *exclusively* to the key processes, improvements to any single process may result in unforeseen problems in related processes within the value stream. This is a critical problem experienced by many organizations that undertake process improvement initiatives. A skeletal map of the entire value stream, with detailed mapping of key processes, will help to ensure that individual process improvements don't have negative effects on other processes.

A map of XYZ's service/repair value stream is shown in Figure 9.3. This is a partial map of the service/repair value stream. The three candidate processes for Six Sigma projects are highlighted on the map. One other analysis should be conducted.

Understanding possible linkages between the three processes is necessary. Problems that might show up in the repair process may be attributable to problems in either the scheduling or diagnostics process. For example, is a slow repair time due solely to the repair process itself or is it also due to parts supply? Similarly, a wrong diagnosis would also retard the repair process. While tools exist within the Six Sigma discipline to perform the requisite analyses, there is no substitute for common sense. Failure to understand the connectivity among these processes could mean that Six Sigma is focusing on a symptom rather than a root-cause problem.

While the emphasis of the analysis has been on those processes that, in this case, can break Company XYZ out of a parity position with Competitor 3, Six Sigma can also identify those non-value-adding costs that are embedded within the repair process, the diagnostic/inspection process, and/or the parts supply process. This is best done during the mapping stage of the Six Sigma project. There is little doubt that these processes are home to waste, in terms of dollars, time, and human activity. Uncovering this waste provides the organization with potentially greater pricing freedom and certainly greater bottom-line impact.

# ESTABLISH PRIORITIES FOR LEAN OR SIX SIGMA PROJECTS

During the course of developing the value stream map, the mapping team will identify specific activities, decision points, or inspection points that are problematic, either because they serve as impediments to value creation and delivery or because they contribute to unnecessary (non-value-adding) costs. As each of these problems is identified on the value map, their potential impact on value delivery and cost should be evaluated in order to establish priorities for lean or Six Sigma projects. An example of such an evaluation is shown in Table 9.4.

This analysis serves as a preliminary evaluation of costs and benefits associated with process improvements. Those costs and benefits will be further incorporated as part of the "benchmarking" process within either lean or Six Sigma planning. Mapping teams typically identify as many as 15 to 30 problems areas across two to three processes within a value stream. It would be foolhardy to attempt to address all those at once. The most rational basis for establishing priorities is to evaluate the impact of each problem on the CTQ factor and on cost. Improved performance on a CTQ will translate into an improved competitive value proposition. This is the strategic implication of process improvements, resulting in enhancements to value creation and delivery and subsequent increases in market share. The elimination of non-value-adding costs enables the organization to translate those improvements into strategic price reductions or to enhance profitability, or both.

The example in Table 9.4, drawn from our forklift planning team, demonstrates two types of opportunities available to the team. In the case of missing tools (map reference point 12), there's an opportunity to apply lean's "5 S" process: sort, set in order, shine, standardize, sustain (this is one Americanized variation on the original Japanese 5 S's). This lean process is designed to bring order out of chaos in the work environment, and is clearly applicable to the problem at hand. Achieving the objective of reducing drive train repair times by 2.5 hours is directly related to a key performance crite-

**Table 9.4** Process improvement opportunities.

| Product/ Market: lift trucks/ warehousing | | Value stream: drive train repairs | Process: shop repair | Team: | Date: 4/20/2005 |
|---|---|---|---|---|---|
| **Problem** | **Map Ref** | **Impact on CTQ** | **Impact on Cost** | **Opportunity** | **Objective** |
| Delay in repair due to missing tools/tools in another location. | #12 | Delays of up to 3 hours per repair. Impacts an average of 28 repairs/ month. | Average repair delay of 2.5 hours × 2 men @ $24/hr × 28 repairs/ month × 12 months = $40,320/yr Lost tools = $12K/yr Total Cost = $52.320 | Conduct a lean 5S to clean up repair bays with correct tools in proper locations at all times. | No repair delays due to missing tools. Reduce average drive train repair time by 2.5 hours. |
| Over-ordering of parts in service dept to ensure adequate supply during repair. Failure to promptly return/account for extra parts. | #17 | Demonstrates lack of skill in diagnostics/ knowledge of service technicians. Significant invoicing delays due to parts unaccounted for. | Approx $800/ repair in extra parts ordered. Restocking delays trigger auto parts order system. Est current excess inventory = $250,000 | Conduct DMAIC to reduce variation from parts required for repair. | Attain 4 Sigma parts orders from service w/in 12 months. Reduce restocking costs by 80%. Customer invoice w/in 48 hours of repair. |

rion of the dealer service CTQ factor. This is the strategic impetus for an effective application of lean tools.

The second problem identified in Table 9.4, creating a "safety net" in the service department by over-ordering parts required for a repair, represents a classic opportunity for a Six Sigma project. Clearly, there is a finite and specific number of parts required for each drive train repair. Variations in parts orders from the required amount represent "defects." In this case, those defects come at a hefty cost to XYZ. Not only are there the restocking costs associated with returning parts to the warehouse, but XYZ has an automated parts ordering system with its OEM (original equipment manufacturer). When a part is ordered, whether by the service department for a repair or by the parts department for a sale, that order triggers an order for a replacement part. By the time the "extra part" is returned from the service department for a credit, the new part is typically en route from the manufacturer, resulting in artificially high inventory levels. Moreover, because the billing department must always check to be sure the part was actually not used before invoicing the customer, those invoices are frequently delayed, resulting in customer perceptions of incompetence and extra cash pressures for XYZ. This represents an opportunity to apply the Six Sigma tools of DMAIC (define, measure, analyze, improve, control).

This is the bridge point between competitive market planning and strategically informed process improvements. From a competitive market planning standpoint, we have identified strategically important product/markets for focused customer value analysis, and have used customer perspectives on value creation and delivery to target key competitors and to develop a strategy to either (a) close the value gap with the value leader, or (b) expand the gap to enhance our leadership position. Either type of strategy requires changes in the organization's value creation and delivery processes. The challenge is to ensure that those changes are driven by critical-to-quality (CTQ) factors *as defined by customers in the targeted market.* The process described in this Chapter actually goes two steps beyond that challenge by (1) assessing the gaps in value performance and setting evaluative priorities based on the importance of those value gaps, and (2) assessing impediments to value creation and delivery within the organization's key processes and setting improvement priorities based on their impact. At this point, the tools of lean (5 S and others) or the tools of Six Sigma (DMAIC and others) can be applied to achieve the improvements required.

# 10

# Monitoring Plan Effectiveness

The development of appropriate monitoring systems is one of those things that every organization talks about, but few actually undertake. The emphasis here is on *appropriate* monitoring systems—measures that provide immediate and constant feedback on progress *and* continually direct attention to the goals of the organization. No one denies the need to track sales, revenue, profitability, and market share, but these are the *outcomes* of providing superior customer value. Financial measures provide no *guidance* for business improvements; they are the *result* of business improvements. And the business improvements that provide the most spectacular financial results are those that focus on enhancing customer value.

One significant benefit of the planning process espoused throughout this book is that if the plan is executed properly, it provides very clear direction for the types of measures that must be put in place. For example, when business performance and marketing mix objectives are properly constructed, they identify precisely what, when, and how much is to be accomplished, as shown in Table 10.1.

These promotion objectives provide clear direction for the type of monitoring systems to be utilized or developed. Some periodic awareness research must be conducted in order to assess unaided/aided awareness. A monitoring system for the evaluation of purchasing intentions must be developed, and the distributor's call reporting system must be designed to track sales calls by market. Similarly, the performance measures identified within the plan's action program provide further direction for the types of monitoring systems required, as shown in Table 10.2.

The final action pertaining to objective 2.1 requires the establishment of baseline data pertaining to repair work completed when promised. Once that baseline has been established and the process improvements carried out, the monitoring system must track ongoing performance of repairs completed when promised.

**Table 10.1** Objectives require monitoring metrics.

**Opportunity 1: Improving awareness of our product and associated services, and improving sales coverage**

Promotion:

1.1 Attain 70% unaided awareness of XYZ as a supplier of forklifts by end of 2006

1.2 Attain 85% unaided awareness of XYZ as a supplier of forklifts by end of 2007

1.3 Attain 95% unaided awareness of XYZ as a supplier of forklifts by end of 2008

1.4 50% of all warehousing customers likely to buy 1 or more forklifts within 1 year will receive a face-to-face sales call once/quarter

1.5 XYZ in on 55% of all forklift deals by end of 2008

Finally, the organization's strategy will dictate certain types of external measures. Our forklift planning team, for example, chose to become "the undisputed value leader" in this targeted product/market. To know whether they are executing that strategy effectively will require the collection of additional market feedback on value delivery.

The old adage "you can't manage what you don't measure" is as relevant today as ever. The challenge lies in identifying the *right* measures in order to evaluate the effectiveness of your competitive marketing plan. The measures that are most relevant to competitive market planning include:

- Objective measures of internal process improvements and cost reductions that are part and parcel of most competitive marketing plans

- Transactional measures reflecting how customers perceive those improvements on a day-to-day basis

- Periodic snapshots of how those improvements are impacting your organization's value proposition *and*

- Financial measures and other business information systems that are aligned with your organization's targeted product/markets

## INTERNAL PERFORMANCE METRICS

These are measures that are calibrated to the specific objectives, actions, and process improvements targeted in the plan. If a key objective is to reduce the number of parts returned to the warehouse from the service department, then the appropriate measure is one that tracks parts orders and parts returned over time. If another objective is to get all repairs completed within the promised number of days, then an objective measure would be one that tracks repair orders and time to completion. Such a monitoring system is illustrated in Figure 10.1. This system was designed to monitor major repairs delivered when promised. The dotted lines indicate the number of days-to-completion promised for each of 30 repairs,

**Table 10.2** Action programs and performance measures.

**Objective 2.1: 95% of service work to be completed on time as promised**

| Actions | Key milestone | Performance measures | Responsibility | Cost |
|---|---|---|---|---|
| Assess performance gaps on CTQ factors relative to Competitor 3 | April 2005 | Performance gaps quantified and rank ordered based on their importance. | John Schimmel | -0- |
| Identify performance gaps relative to Competitor 3 for each performance attribute within the most important CTQ factor | April 2005 | Importance weights established for each performance attribute. | John Schimmel | -0- |
| Flesh out Y Platform to confirm value stream for analysis | May 2005 | $Y = $ #1 CTQ; Sub-Y's $=$ Performance attributes with importance weights. Identification of input processes ($X$'s) affecting the outputs ($Y$'s). | Jim Plummer | -0- |
| Develop and evaluate CTQ/process matrix | May 2005 | Impact of processes on attributes assessed and weights assigned. Processes ranked in terms of impact on quality driver attributes and cost. | Jim Plummer | -0- |
| Develop map of value stream | May 2005 | Skeletal map of complete value stream with swim lanes. Detailed map of priority processes. Problem areas identified. | Roger Lauck | -0- |
| Select/define lean Six Sigma projects | June 2005 | Impact of identified problems on quality driver and on cost assessed. Opportunities and objectives identified. Rank order based on impact. Top 3 opportunities selected. Approval by lean Six Sig sponsor. | Peter Hall | -0- |
| Determine baseline performance criteria | July 2005 | % of work orders with promise dates included. % of completes within promise date. % defects, etc. | John Schimmel | -0- |

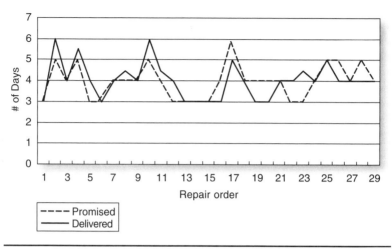

**Figure 10.1** Repair promise/delivery times.

and the solid line indicates the actual number of days required to complete the repair. The graph reveals that 15 repairs were completed within a time frame other than the time frame promised. Even though repairs 19 and 20 were completed in less time than promised, these two repairs nonetheless reflect a deviation from the objective. The warehouse operator *may* be pleased to have the repair completed early, but the early return may well have caused an undesirable disruption to scheduled operations. Therefore, the early completion represents a defect, to use a Six Sigma term.

Obvious as all this seems, we are continually amazed by the number of organizations that fail to have these types of measures in place. Implementing a monitoring system *after* a process has been improved does little to let you evaluate the results of that improvement. Your first indication of the need for a specific monitoring system will occur during the process of documenting the impact of problems identified within your value stream map (Table 9.4). The extent to which these impacts can be readily documented suggests that you have the appropriate monitoring systems in place. Where there is difficulty in documenting a time or cost impact of a problem you will need to design an appropriate monitoring system. That system should be developed and put in place immediately to provide the benchmarking data for future documentation of improvements.

# TRANSACTIONAL MEASURES OF CUSTOMER VALUE

After determining that your process improvements are achieving the intended results on an objective basis, you will want to find out if customers are actually noticing these improvements. And you don't want to wait for the results from your next customer value analysis (CVA), because there may be additional steps required to impact customer perceptions of process improvements—such as a more effective communications program. The good news is that your CVA development process also provides direction for an ongoing transactional measurement system.

The customer value model provides a list of quality drivers, and a list of the attributes (value performance criteria, or VPCs) that comprise them. The gap analyses and the CTQ/process matrix (Table 9.3) led to the identification of specific processes (inputs) having the greatest impact on specific quality drivers and attributes (outputs). Those processes can be linked to specific customer transactions with your organization. The result is a list of attributes (questions) appropriate for measuring customer perceptions of your performance relative to each type of customer transaction.

An effective transactional measurement system should meet several key criteria, including:

- Customer feedback should be easy and inexpensive to collect

- The monitoring system should flag instances of poor performance for immediate corrective action

- The system should provide real-time, dynamic access to reports for all managers, along with the capacity to "slice-and-dice" the data to address a variety of management issues

- The system should include a simple "dashboard-like" overview, along with the capacity to drill down to the appropriate functional issues

## Data Collection

The transactional measurement system should be sufficiently flexible to accommodate a variety of data collection methodologies. Ideally, customer transactions will automatically feed into an Internet- or intranet-based system, which in turn would randomly select transactions for follow-up surveys. The system should also have a built-in capacity to screen transactions to prevent over-surveying of the organization's customers. Surveys could be conducted by phone, using the organization's own personnel to conduct the interviews, or by mail or the Internet, requesting customers to complete the survey at the organization's Web site. The surveys must be brief to minimize respondent burden, and should include only those key questions or attributes identified in the value model. An example of such a telephone-based data collection methodology is shown in Figure 10.2.

This is a transactional survey pertaining to sales calls for a provider of lists and labels, among other services. This company has a call center to handle incoming customer calls, and has dedicated several of its call stations to outgoing, transactional survey calls. The call center employee uses their menu-driven system to select the type of transactional survey to conduct. Customer information is transparently entered onto the employee's computer

| Customer Name | Eric Reidenbach |
|---|---|
| Customer Phone # | 601-334-7479 |
| Customer Company | Market Value Solutions |
| Customer Location | Hattiesburg |
| Customer Interaction Date | 12/6/2004 |
| Product/Service | Lists and Labels |
| Market | Small to Medium Business |
| Surveyor ID | 547832 |
| Survey Type | Sales Call |

Mr. Reidenbach, you were recently in contact with one of our sales representatives. I'd like to ask you to rate the performance of our sales rep on just a few key issues. For each question, please rate our performance on a scale of 1 through 10, with 1 being very poor performance and 10 being excellent performance. Your input about our service will help us to better serve you in the future.

| Please rate our level of performance on the following:<br><br>Courtesy of the sales representative | Very poor | | | | | | | | | Excellent | Not applicable |
|---|---|---|---|---|---|---|---|---|---|---|---|
| | 1 | 2 | 3 | 4 | 5 | 6 | 7 | 6 | 9 | 10 | NA |
| Ability of sales rep to understand the unique and changing demands of your business | 0 | 0 | 0 | 0 | 0 | 0 | 0 | 0 | 0 | 0 | 0 |
| Ability to configure the services to your specifications | 0 | 0 | 0 | 0 | 0 | 0 | 0 | 0 | 0 | 0 | 0 |
| Technical knowledge of the representative | 0 | 0 | 0 | 0 | 0 | 0 | 0 | 0 | 0 | 0 | 0 |
| Responsiveness to solving problems | 0 | 0 | 0 | 0 | 0 | 0 | 0 | 0 | 0 | 0 | 0 |
| Ability of sales rep to answer questions | 0 | 0 | 0 | 0 | 0 | 0 | 0 | 0 | 0 | 0 | 0 |
| Ability to communicate on matters relevant to your business | 0 | 0 | 0 | 0 | 0 | 0 | 0 | 0 | 0 | 0 | 0 |
| Quality of consultative services | 0 | 0 | 0 | 0 | 0 | 0 | 0 | 0 | 0 | 0 | 0 |
| Professionalism of sales personnel | 0 | 0 | 0 | 0 | 0 | 0 | 0 | 0 | 0 | 0 | 0 |
| Competitive pricing | 0 | 0 | 0 | 0 | 0 | 0 | 0 | 0 | 0 | 0 | 0 |
| Availability of pricing programs that met your needs | 0 | 0 | 0 | 0 | 0 | 0 | 0 | 0 | 0 | 0 | 0 |
| Terms and conditions | 0 | 0 | 0 | 0 | 0 | 0 | 0 | 0 | 0 | 0 | 0 |
| Overall value of sales support provided | 0 | 0 | 0 | 0 | 0 | 0 | 0 | 0 | 0 | 0 | 0 |

**Figure 10.2** Transactional survey.

screen, and the appropriate survey appears on the screen. The employee simply reads the script, clicking on the appropriate response as provided by the customer, then clicks "submit" to include the survey data in the continually evolving dataset. This is a simple and inexpensive system managed entirely through the organization's intranet.

## Responsiveness

Customers don't mind responding to short surveys like this, provided they are assured that their responses are being heard. There's nothing worse for a business than to solicit customer input and then fail to act on it promptly. For that reason, your transactional measurement system should have a "red flag" component built into it that will immediately alert the appropriate manager to take action when a customer reports a poor experience. In today's electronic world, that function is easily designed such that a rating of, say, 4 or lower on a 10 point scale will immediately trigger an e-mail to the appropriate manager. Responses to customer ratings of poor performance can be much more effective if the transactional measurement system is linked to the organization's CRM system, as shown in Figure 10.3.

This linkage provides the ultimate in customer relationship management. The organization's CRM system provides critical information about each customer's economic value to the organization, while the transactional measurement system provides critical information about the organization's value to each customer. The objective, of course, is to maximize your organization's creation and delivery of value to your most economically valuable customers. Instant "red flag" alerts for poor performance, when linked to the organization's CRM system, enable managers to take the most appropriate remedial action in the most timely manner.

## Real-Time Reporting

In order for the transactional measurement system to have real utility, it must include a reporting capability that is easy to use and accessible by all members of the management team. Accessibility is especially important for members of the planning team and any Six Sigma Black Belts and Green Belts involved in process improvements. These team members want and need this sort of customer feedback in order to effectively monitor customer-perceived performance changes attributable to process improvements. One example of an easy-to-use, menu-driven reporting system is shown in Figures 10.4 and 10.5.

Consistent with the emphasis on a strategic focus throughout this book, the reporting system should be capable of generating reports on a product/market basis. It makes no sense to target a strategically important group of customers in the development of a competitive plan, and then lump all customers together when analyzing trends or making other comparisons. The

| Customer information | |
|---|---|
| Customer name | Eric Reidenbach |
| Customer location | Hattiesburg |
| Customer company | Market Value Solutions |
| Customer phone number | 601-334-7479 |

| Lifetime value | |
|---|---|
| Annual list revenue | $$$$ |
| Support services | $$$$ |
| Related products | $$$$ |
| Est LTV (10 years) | $$$$$ |

| Transaction information | |
|---|---|
| Customer number | sh6040 |
| Survey type | SUR 1 |
| Location | Region 4 |
| Action date | 12/8/2004 |
| Dealing w/product | Lists & labels |
| Market | Small/med Business |

| Survey information | |
|---|---|
| Surveyors code | 547832 |
| Survey date | 12/8/2005 |
| Survey type | Sales |

| Customer survey | |
|---|---|
| Courtesy of the sales representative | 3 |
| Ability of sales rep to understand the unique and changing demands of your business | 6 |
| Ability to configure the services to your specifications | 6 |
| Technical knowledge of the representative | 5 |
| Responsiveness to solving problems | 5 |
| Ability of sales rep to answer questions | 6 |
| Ability to communicate on matters relevant to your business | 3 |
| Quality of consultative services | 6 |
| Professionalism of sales personnel | 6 |
| Competitive pricing | 6 |
| Availability of pricing programs that met your needs | 6 |
| Terms and conditions | 7 |
| Overall value of sales support provided | 5 |

Ratings that produced red flags

**Figure 10.3**   Survey linkage to CRM.

monitoring systems must be as strategically focused as the competitive planning system.

## "Dashboard" Overview

Managers generally prefer to see the "big picture" at a glance, then drill down to specifics as necessary. For that reason, it can be very beneficial to have a "dashboard" type of report, as shown in Figure 10.6. The easier it is

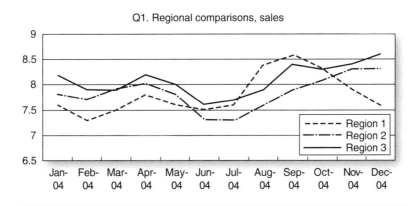

---

Trend report

Choose from the choices below to customize your query

Report on Day ☐ / ☐ / ☐    Report from 01 / 01 / 04 to 12 / 31 / 04

(For today's report leave blank)        Enter Date Format mm/dd/yy

---

Q# [ 1 ▼]

Market [ Small to medium business ▼]

Dealing with Product [ Lists and labels ▼]

---

Choose only ONE of the Following three location sub-dividers

At location [ LOCATION 1 ▼]

In region [ All ▼]

In group [ All ▼]

[ Generate Report ]

---

**Figure 10.4**   Menu-driven reporting system.

Q1. Regional comparisons, sales

Region 1
Region 2
Region 3

Jan-04  Feb-04  Mar-04  Apr-04  May-04  Jun-04  Jul-04  Aug-04  Sep-04  Oct-04  Nov-04  Dec-04

**Figure 10.5**   Performance trend report.

for managers to use the reporting system, the more they are likely to use it, which benefits the entire organization. This type of report shows overall changes in performance from month to month or week to week in the center of the image. Changes in "red flag" performance can be seen on the left, and performance by functional area (parts, service, and so on) is shown on the right. From this general overview, the interested manager can drill down by geographic area, by product, by market, by functional area, and by specific periods of time.

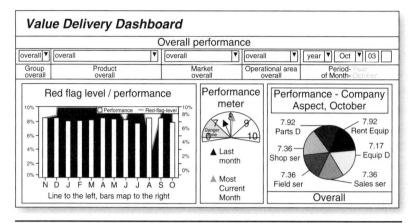

**Figure 10.6**  Management dashboard.

The two things that this sort of reporting system provides are (1) ease of use (menu driven with drill-down capabilities) and timeliness (real-time interactivity). These are the conditions most managers require if they are to use the monitoring system effectively.

# DIAGNOSTIC SNAPSHOTS

Of course, the information you receive from your transactional measurement system is based on the perceptions of your customers only. In order to avoid the same kind of "market myopia" promulgated by some customer satisfaction advocates, you must periodically check the "temperature" of the entire market(s) that you are targeting with your product(s). However, these diagnostic measures can be conducted very effectively and efficiently in view of the fact that your initial customer value analysis has already revealed the true drivers of quality and value, and the attributes that comprise them.

By way of illustration, a value model from the utilities industry is provided in Figure 10.7. The focus of this model is residential users of electricity. This value model includes four quality drivers and two subcomponents of image. The model is very robust, with an $R^2$ of .92. Included within the quality, image, and price drivers are 50 individual attributes, such as those shown in Table 10.3 for routine transactions.

These attributes or VPCs are listed in the order of their "importance" to routine transactions, based on results of the factor analysis conducted during the initial CVA. The large number of attributes included in the initial CVA was necessary in order to ensure capturing the essence of what customers mean by "value" within any given product/market. However, once the model has been developed and verified as robust, subsequent measures of customer value can be conducted with a limited subset of two or three at-

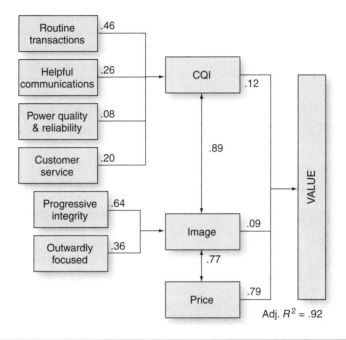

**Figure 10.7** Electricity/residential users value model.

---

**Table 10.3** "Routine transactions" attributes.

- Provides bills that are easy to understand
- Provides information about changes in prices, service options, and regulations
- Ease of scheduling nonemergency service at my home at a time convenient for me
- Provides bills with helpful info about my energy use
- Provides bills with sufficient detail for my needs
- Ease of contact for nonemergency information or service
- Ease of correcting billing problems
- Communicates to me about changes in billing and billing options
- Provides accurate bills
- Provides help for people w/finance troubles paying bills
- Provides complete information or service when requested

---

tributes representing each driver. In this case, the top three attributes from each value and quality driver were utilized. In other words, this utility company is now able to "diagnose" the status of its relative value proposition on an annual basis, using just 21 performance attributes. This has resulted in considerable cost savings with less respondent fatigue. Whenever the utility company discovers declining performance on one of its quality drivers, it can do a deeper dive in order to determine the precise nature of that decline. This "deeper dive" can be done by resurveying on the single quality driver using all the original attributes, or it can be done on a more qualitative basis with focus groups.

# ALIGNMENT OF BUSINESS INFORMATION SYSTEMS

The final arbiter of plan effectiveness is business performance results. The effectiveness of the competitive marketing plan will ultimately be assessed on the basis of the product/market objectives (market share, revenue, profit, and so on) specified within the plan. The challenge facing most companies in monitoring these performance outcomes is a matter of aligning their business reporting systems with their targeted product/markets.

Many organizations have operated with either a production or sales orientation for many years. As a result, their financial accounting and other business information systems are structured along product lines and/or functional areas of the business. It is not uncommon, when first attempting to develop and analyze a product/market matrix, for the organization to discover that it has the data to plug into the "totals" column for product lines, but that they are unable to allocate those totals by market segment. This inability to track financial or market share performance by product/market will have serious consequences if not corrected. The most significant consequence is that, without the ability to track performance by product/market, no one in the organization can be held accountable for business objectives at the product/market level. And, absent that accountability, these competitive marketing plans will simply reside on some manager's shelf, dusted off annually for appearance's sake.

Realignment of the organization's business information systems is no small matter, but it must be tackled at the earliest possible opportunity. The lack of such realignment is one among several impediments to effective plan deployment to be discussed further in the next Chapter.

# Part III:
# Competitive Planning Deployment

## Chapter 11
Fourteen Keys to Successful Deployment

## Chapter 12
Competing For Customers

# 11

# Fourteen Keys to Successful Deployment

The previous 10 Chapters of this book have described a comprehensive framework for developing a value-based, market-driven competitive planning system. The successful deployment of such a comprehensive system for value management requires vision, commitment, leadership, a passion for customers, and an overarching belief that customers will consistently seek and buy those products and services that provide the best value.

We know that most business organizations collect customer feedback of one sort or another regarding their products and services. But the question we hear from managers most frequently is, "Now that I have this information, what do I do with it? How do I use it to improve my unit's performance?" We believe there are many reasons why this is such a prevalent question, some of which have to do with the type of information collected in the first place, some having to do with how that information is analyzed and disseminated, and some having to do with confusion regarding whether customer information of this sort should be used as part of a management control system (a report card), a tactical change system, or a more strategic customer learning system.

A 2002 benchmarking study of both industrial and service organizations that routinely collect customer information, conducted by the American Productivity and Quality Center (APQC), revealed that less than 36 percent of U.S. businesses believe that they do an "adequate job" (defined as a rating of 7 or better on a scale of 1 to 10) of deploying that information strategically, and less than 30 percent report that they "adequately" deploy that information tactically. Less that 26 percent reported adequate linkages to any sort of business performance. (APQC, 2002). A 2005 study of customer information utilization, sponsored by the Marketing Science Institute, revealed that only 24 percent of the firms studied utilized their customer feedback information *both* as a control mechanism and as strategic input. Fully 46 percent of companies studied utilized customer feedback solely as a report card, and 16 percent only collected customer feedback on an *ad hoc* basis, not using the customer information for any systematic purposes (Morgan et al., 2005).

We believe that the tools described throughout this book will help your organization to effectively deploy a powerful, comprehensive system of market value measurement and management that will enable you to achieve a sustainable, differential value advantage in those product/markets in which you choose to compete. We also know that if your organization is similar to many with which we work, you will confront numerous obstacles to the successful deployment of this market value management system. Accordingly we offer 14 suggestions to overcome those obstacles. These 14 suggestions are based on factors that separate and differentiate those organizations that have effectively deployed this competitive planning system from those that have not. Eight of these are critical to success in the early stages of deployment. They include:

1. Identify an effective corporate champion

2. Don't measure unless you plan to manage

3. Be sure of your strategic focus

4. Let customers decide what questions to ask

5. Select reliable research vendors

6. Understand the needs of internal customers

7. Effectively utilize multifunctional teams

8. Reward employee contributions

Another six will help to ensure a successful deployment over the longer term:

9. Get the organization beyond a technological perspective on value

10. Activate the discipline of Six Sigma, and integrate disparate corporate initiatives

11. Ensure accountability through monthly performance reviews

12. Continually evaluate the fit of competitive marketing plans with the corporate growth strategy

13. Develop a structure to support the strategy

14. Manage culture change

# SHORT-TERM KEYS TO SUCCESSFUL DEPLOYMENT

There are a number of short-term issues that if overlooked or circumvented will likely derail the engine of customer value management before it moves very far down the track. We will address eight of these in this section.

## 1. Corporate Champion

Every business manager will appreciate that any new corporate initiative will have a greater chance of success if supported by the CEO or COO of the organization. But one who "champions" an initiative does more than merely support it. A champion is *passionate* about the role of value creation and delivery in the attainment of a sustainable competitive advantage, *systematic and disciplined* in applying the tools of customer value to competitive market planning, and *inspirational* in getting others in the organization to follow the lead. Such a person need not actually be the CEO or COO, but must have the confidence of that person and must be empowered to bring others on board.

The old maxim, "if you really want to get the job done, get the busiest person in the organization to do it," may or may not apply here. Some managers make themselves busy by constantly putting out fires. They may become valued in the organization for their ability to quickly solve a great many problems, but they may not have the single-minded focus on the end-game to serve as an effective champion. The effective deployment of customer value management requires a steadfast commitment to strategic focus, an insistence that every business decision be supported by the voice of customer value, and the use of appropriate metrics to monitor progress toward value leadership.

An effective corporate champion will also move quickly to institutionalize a customer value culture. That person will ensure that the voice of customer value is readily and easily heard and understood throughout the organization, and that progress toward value leadership is cogent and ongoing. One customer value champion managed to change the corporate vision to one based on value, then made sure that every employee in the organization understood the importance of that vision as it related to his or her specific job. This institutionalization of a customer value culture ensures that the entire initiative will not die with a change in personnel. Obviously, this also requires a unique sort of champion, one who puts the organization ahead of an ego.

## 2. Don't Measure Unless You Plan to Manage

We referred earlier to the old maxim, "You can't manage what you don't measure." But there's a corollary to that maxim, which is, "Don't bother to measure if you don't plan to manage." Measuring market definitions and perceptions of value is a resource commitment, and every such investment should generate a good return. But merely measuring market perceptions of value will do nothing to change those perceptions. The only thing that will change your competitive value proposition is if you or one of your competitors changes some aspect of how you/they do business. And, if you are doing nothing to manage your competitive value proposition, then your competitors are effectively managing it for you.

Many organizations are initially intrigued by the tools of customer value analysis—they make a great deal of intuitive sense! Managers want to be market driven, and these tools provide a true market perspective on value creation and delivery. Acknowledging that, the organization's management team will often decide to "stick their toe in the water," making the commitment to conduct a customer value analysis or two. Upon receiving the results, they either (a) congratulate themselves on being an outstanding value provider and believe that will continue, or (b) grouse because they are not in an enviable value position, but hope that it will be better if they decide to measure again next year, or (c) denigrate the validity and veracity of the information. This is a terrible waste of corporate resources! Why would you invest the time and money to collect and analyze customer data if you were not planning simultaneously to either (a) leverage any value advantages you may have, or (b) address value disadvantages in order to move toward value leadership?

A B2B telecommunications firm made precisely this mistake. Its management team became enamored with the tools of CVA, and made the financial commitment to measure market perceptions of value on an annual basis. In fact, that group of managers was so committed to the notion of customer value as a driving business force that they linked management compensation to changes in their value ratings. Now, it would seem obvious that if employee compensation is tied to changes in value ratings, employees will work to improve those ratings. And they probably did—each in his or her own way. But the organization made no further investment in the *systematic* development of a competitive marketing plan based on this information. Hence, there was no business-wide plan to enhance value performance. And, of course, employees were very unhappy with the lack of bonus checks at the end of the year! In their minds, it was not the lack of follow through that produced a lack of change, it was the measures.

The lesson to learn from this illustration is to not embark on a program to measure customer value if you have not also made the commitment to systematically develop and implement a competitive plan to profitably increase market share based on superior value delivery. Market feedback on value performance can be an incredibly powerful strategic tool, which means that the investment in collecting and analyzing that information should generate substantial returns. But that simply won't happen if your organization is among the 62 percent identified by Morgan et al. (2005) who either use customer feedback as merely a report card or don't use it at all. Before you invest in measuring it, be sure you have the commitment to manage it!

## 3. Strategic Focus

When embarking on the road toward competitive planning of the sort discussed here, many organizations recognize that different markets will define value differently with respect to different products. The logic is too compelling to ignore. But this does not necessarily mean that most organizations will identify markets or product lines appropriately, nor does it necessarily mean that most organizations will focus on the *right* product/markets.

We are often surprised by the number of organizations that continue to define product lines from an internal perspective, or that incorrectly identify the markets they serve. Like the term *value,* the terms *markets* and *market segments* have taken on such a generic meaning that managers toss them around without much consideration for the meaning they are intended to convey. We have heard references to "the locomotive market," the "backhoe market," the "mortgage market" and others from managers in a variety of industries. We have seen organizations define market segments in terms of customer size, only to learn that "size" is defined by the amount of revenue those customers spend with the client company alone. And we have seen market segments defined on some attitudinal basis that defies the accurate categorization of customers into segments. Of course, we have also seen markets defined in terms of "historical traditions," many of which have little relationship to customer purchasing behavior. Any such fundamental flaw in the identification of products and markets will produce a flawed and misleading perspective on market value.

The other problem in attaining strategic focus is the lack of data pertaining to the selected criteria for setting strategic priorities. We have mentioned repeatedly the problem of business information systems that are structured around product and functional perspectives, rather than being structured around market perspectives. The lack of objective data on a product/market basis can lead to erroneous conclusions about which product/markets are strategically most important. Even if the organization's current information system cannot provide data at the appropriate level of resolution, a systematic effort should be made to allocate revenue and market share data across the product/market matrix in order to avoid a serious and costly error based on someone's personal agenda. No company can be truly market-focused unless it has the information to attain that focus.

## 4. Rely on Customers for the Right Questions

Companies that have relied on the metrics of customer satisfaction for a decade or more generally began that initiative by getting a group of managers together to generate a list of survey questions. These may be updated annually, but there is typically no basis for determining whether these are even the right questions to be asking. And companies that embark on the customer value journey are at risk of making the same mistake.

The questionnaire(s) developed for an effective customer value analysis should be comprised of questions generated by customers, not managers. This requires conducting some qualitative research in the targeted product/markets in order to find out what those questions should be. Typically, a couple focus groups conducted with your customers and those of your competitors will serve the purpose. In some business situations, individual interviews may be required. It is important to do your homework.

The greatest difficulty with qualitative research to generate survey questions is to remain focused on the objective. This is not the time to ascertain what your competitive value proposition is. Nor are you trying to get customers to compare you with competition. The objective of these focus groups is to generate a comprehensive list of questions that will result in a robust value model. The robustness of the resulting model for each product/market ($R^2$), along with the actionability of driver attributes, is the ultimate test of the extent to which you have adequately captured the market's definition of value.

Does this mean that you will need to scrap all the survey questions and the associated tracking data you have already acquired? Emphatically, *no!* The transition to customer value is evolutionary, not revolutionary. Many questions from your current customer information system will remain as part of your value models, and key tracking questions may also be retained. But getting customer input into the content of your questionnaires is critical for the development of valid and reliable value models, which in turn are essential for the development of effective competitive marketing plans. By the way, having the relevant managers observe the actual focus groups, or tapes of them, can go a long way toward aligning the external and internal mental models of value.

## 5. Reliable Research Vendors

Although some companies maintain a market research capability internally, most organizations will outsource the data collection and analyses that will drive their customer value management initiatives. And there are certainly a great many options available from which to choose. While it is not the purpose of this book to detail the criteria for vendor selection, there are a few key questions that will help ensure the selection of a reliable vendor.

Since the mid-1990s, when customer value management made its debut, many research companies that historically conducted customer satisfaction research began to advertise that they now conduct customer value research as well. Their claim to legitimacy often consisted of little more than adding a value question to their existing surveys. Answers to the following questions should provide some guidance in selecting an appropriate research firm:

- Is your research typically focused on specific product/markets?
  - The 2002 APQC benchmarking study on the deployment of customer information demonstrated conclusively that companies employing a strategic focus in their data collection and analysis were significantly and substantially more effective in utilizing that information throughout the organization (APQC, 2005).

- Do you acquire a market perspective on value, or just our customer's perspective?
  - Since value is a relative dynamic, it would seem obvious that a market perspective on value will have more strategic utility than just the perspective of one's own customers. Yet, of the 37 companies studied by Morgan et al., only 4 of those collected data from competitors' customers (Morgan et al., 2005).

- Do you use multiple attributes to measure the constructs of value, price, image, and the several quality drivers? Do you provide evidence of the reliability of the drivers?
  - Only 38 percent of companies in the MSI (Marketing Science Institute) sponsored research used any form of multivariate analysis, and most were limited to regression approaches. Managers in firms that use the more sophisticated analyses report that much deeper and actionable insights are realized through those analyses (Morgan et al., 2005). Unless the vendor uses multiple attributes for each value and quality driver, they will not generally be able to provide any evidence of model reliability, a necessary condition for model validity.

- Are the quality drivers generated empirically (that is, from the data) or intuitively?
  - Absent the empirical identification of quality drivers, the vendor will be able to provide no evidence of the structural validity of those drivers.

- Do your analyses account for the interaction of quality, price, and image?
  - Many vendors merely provide means, frequencies, and trend lines for attribute-level and overall satisfaction or value scores (Morgan et al., 2005). To the extent that vendors go beyond this level of reporting, they are often limited to simple bi-variate correlations among the attributes. (for a more complete explanation of the problems associated with this approach, see Appendix A, Technical Notes on Value Measurement)

- What evidence do you provide of the validity of your value models?
  - Value models should result in a minimum $R^2$ of .75 if they are to be used to drive strategic initiatives. There should also be substantial evidence that higher scores on value produce higher levels of customer loyalty and lower levels of price sensitivity.

## 6. Understand Needs of Internal Customers

An organization usually generates customer value data in one particular department of the firm, typically some division within market research. However, employees using that information generally reside in other departments. These are the "customers" of the CVA products. As one manager put it, "Measurement doesn't change anything, people change things . . . so you have to make sure you get the [customer] data in the hands of whoever may be able to use it" (Morgan et al., 2005). The meaningful dissemination of customer value information to those internal customers is critical to the effective utilization of that information, whether for tactical, strategic, or benchmarking purposes. Additionally, the outputs of strategic and competitive planning—the identification of strategically targeted product/markets and the basis for that targeting, the strategies for each of those product/markets, the specific marketing mix objectives, and the process improvement targets—should be readily accessible to all who have any responsibility for the execution of those strategies. This type of "open information system" will contribute significantly to successful deployment of the competitive planning system.

More important than simply having information available, however, is the need for understanding its importance, being able to use it effectively, and identifying the specific ways in which each employee contributes to the overall creation and delivery of value. Again, Morgan et al. (2005) report that they found three important aspects to the dissemination of customer information: frequency, vertical and horizontal dissemination, and recipient perceptions. The more frequently customer feedback is disseminated throughout the organization, the more employees will recognize the importance of customer input to the attainment of the organization's business objectives. Certainly, the periodic CVA results should be widely distributed throughout the organization. But the deployment of a transactional measurement system, such as the one described in Chapter 10, will further increase the frequency of information dissemination.

Vertical dissemination refers to the degree to which customer information is distributed up and down throughout the organization's hierarchy, and horizontal dissemination refers to the distribution of customer information across functional areas of the organization. One large distributor of earth-moving equipment that has successfully deployed a competitive planning system reports that both its customer feedback (CVA and transactional survey results) and the uses to which such feedback are put are broadly disseminated throughout the organization. Customer value analyses are conducted in key product/markets annually, and the findings are discussed with small groups of employees throughout the company as part of their continuing employee development program. Managers in every functional area of the organization have access to the Web-based transactional measurement system, and track performance within their functional area daily. Those managers also provide weekly progress reports to front-line employees. Competitive market plans are posted on the company's intranet, and are accessible to all managers. Value stream maps are also posted on the intranet but, more importantly, they are used for training purposes in the service and parts departments, and are prominently displayed in the company's lunch room, with dry-erase markers conveniently located for employee comments. The managing director of this company recognizes the importance of keeping all employees informed of the strategic initiatives for which they are responsible, and also recognizes that competitive market strategies must be openly communicated both internally and externally.

"Recipient perceptions" refer to the perceived characteristics of the customer value information to internal customers. This is often the source of the most significant impediment to the successful deployment of a competitive planning system, and is one of the reasons for so much attention to deployment key 5. There are three key features of a customer value measurement and reporting system that will significantly impact user perceptions of its utility. The first pertains to the clarity and believability of the information, the second pertains to the usability of that information, and the third has to do with the managerial actionability of the information.

The first condition for positive recipient perceptions of customer value information is that the information must be demonstrably believable. Some might say that the information must be accurate; the technical terminology is that the information must be both reliable and valid. The first reaction of many old-school managers can be summarized by the comment of a vice president in a financial services firm who said, "Those customers don't know what they're talking about." The only way to counter this kind of response, other than recognizing that this manager would serve you better by working for a competitor, is to be able to provide empirical evidence of both the reliability and the validity of the information. This sort of evidence is readily available if using the type of analytical tools described in this book.

The second condition for positive recipient perceptions is usability. In many situations, customer information is reported in such a convoluted collection of graphs, charts, and tables that no manager can figure out what the information is telling them. As one manager put it, "Don't try to tell me what this says. Just tell me what to do." The four very simple tools of CVA make the customer value information readily accessible to every employee in the organization. Sometimes, too, the timeliness of information will have a negative impact on its usability. Who wants to try to fix a customer problem three months after the customer has reported it? A transactional measurement system with real-time "red flag" capabilities will prevent that type of problem.

Finally, the customer value information must have clear diagnostic implications for managerial action. A customer information system that doesn't clearly indicate which are the most important issues to address does not provide the appropriate direction for managers. "Drivers" that lack detailed performance criteria provide little direction for actionability. What does the manager change when informed that the organization is performing poorly on "responsiveness," and there are no additional performance criteria to clarify what "responsiveness" means?

Internal customers require information that is reliable, valid, timely, understandable, diagnostic, and actionable. They need to know what strategic imperatives caused the organization to collect and analyze this information in the first place, and they need to know their specific role in impacting positive change in the creation and delivery of value.

## 7. Effective Utilization of Multifunctional Teams

Any manager who has participated in any sort of executive development program and, especially, any manager who has attended virtually any business school in the last 15 years has probably heard more than he or she cares to about the importance of team building and the tearing down of institutional silos. And, while we certainly support the elimination of cross-functional institutional barriers of any sort by any means, we advocate the use of multifunctional planning teams for a far more practical reason: successfully implementing the product/market strategies and holding people accountable for execution of the relevant actions.

The customer value models we have seen over the past 10 years are rarely limited to a single quality driver, one that might be actionable exclusively within a single functional area of the organization. Most models involve elements of equipment or service delivery, service or service support, product development or improvements, or various aspects of communication. In other words, the market value opportunities that emerge from most customer value models are not unidimensional, they are multidimensional, and the resulting strategies entail deployment of the full marketing mix up and down the entire value delivery stream. That said, it would be irresponsible to constitute a planning team consisting of managers from a single functional area (for example, manufacturing). How would managers in the service department react if they were simply presented a competitive marketing plan that called for a 50 percent improvement in repair turnaround times, accompanied by a 10 percent reduction in costs—all without any direct involvement of a service manager on the planning team? We could go on, but the point is probably clear. In order to fully capitalize on the value-enhancing opportunities that emerge from a customer value analysis, managers from all relevant functional areas of the organization must be directly involved in development of the competitive marketing plan that will take advantage of those opportunities.

Then there is the matter of accountability. Action programs include milestones, performance measures, and points of responsibility. Those points of responsibility *must* be resident within the planning team itself. Individual work plans pertaining to key actions may well be delegated to another employee within the manager's functional area, but the actual point of accountability must reside with the planning team. As will be discussed shortly, each competitive marketing plan should be reviewed on a periodic basis, preferably monthly. It simply wouldn't do for someone on the team to report, "Well, I assigned that responsibility to someone else, but I don't know whether they got the job done." Nor will it be very effective for different members of the planning team to each say, "I thought you were going to do that." The responsible party from the relevant functional area must be an accountable member of the planning team.

## 8. Reward Employees for Their Contributions

One reason employees often resist change, or new organizational initiatives such as that proposed here, is that any enthusiasm for the change will typically result in more work with no additional compensation. Indeed, we have been directly involved with many competitive planning initiatives in which managers and other employees throughout the organization were instructed to participate on planning teams or process improvement initiatives that required two to four dedicated days of employee time. Those employees were often quite enthusiastic about the opportunity, and many even saw the opportunity as a means to career advancement, until they realized that their participation came *in addition to,* rather than *in place of,* their regular responsibilities.

Although it's true that many managers recognize that this sort of market-driven, systematic approach to value enhancement will ultimately make their jobs easier and more rewarding, the organization that is really committed to deploying this approach successfully will provide interim rewards to employees responsible for making the deployment a success. These rewards need not take the form of salary increases or bonuses, but may be as simple as arranging a night out or a weekend of relaxation for the employee and companion of choice. The point is that simple expressions of gratitude for an important contribution can go a long way toward a successful competitive planning deployment.

There are, of course, many more complex incentive programs that might be used, and the creative champion will find quite a variety of useful resources. Our contention is that a little can go a long way if the action is thoughtful, meaningful, and sincerely delivered.

# KEYS TO SUCCESS FOR THE LONG HAUL

The suggestions just provided will help ensure the successful launch of your organization's customer value management system, and the development and deployment of competitive marketing plans for competing for customers and winning with value. These suggestions are derived from the success stories of numerous organizations and the proactive creativity of their management teams.

## 9. Move the Organization beyond a Technological View of Value

We have worked with organizations in the manufacturing sector, including both industrial and consumer, as well as organizations in the services sector, including utilities, health care, telecommunications, financial services, and a host of others. One common thread we have observed is that many organizations persist in taking a technological perspective on value creation and delivery, as opposed to a customer or competitive perspective. That is, they persist in the belief that all value is created within the product or service itself, and fail to understand that value at the point of production does not necessarily equal value at the point of consumption. Unfortunately, many academic proponents of customer value contribute to this perception by emphasizing the measurement of "value in use" or "value-based pricing." The upshot of this reductionistic view of customer value is that when developing competitive marketing plans, many of these organizations rely solely on their ability to change the technological features of their products and services and fail to address the actual delivery of those products and services through their distributors, brokers, branches, and so on. Even when organizations acknowledge the contribution of their channels of distribution, they often assume that they can simply dictate what those distributors should do differently.

One of the most important steps any corporation can take to ensure the successful deployment of their customer value initiative is to involve representatives from their channels of distribution in the actual development of their competitive marketing plans. Most value models across industries will include some quality drivers pertaining to installation, service, problem solving, or some other personal interface with customers that is handled by a distributor, sales agency, branch, or broker. Just as it makes little sense for a marketing manager to set objectives and develop action programs for a service manager without that manager's direct involvement, it also makes little sense for a corporate planning team to dictate objectives and actions for its distribution channel without direct representation from that channel.

There is often a "we/they," or "us and them" divide between a manufacturer and its dealers/distributors, between a bank and its branches, or between an insurance company and its brokers. One manufacturer of agricultural equipment has driven this divide to new levels, failing to include dealers in the development of any strategic initiatives, changing pricing programs on a completely ad hoc basis, and generally doing just about anything in its power to communicate to dealers that they are to be totally subservient to the will of the "800-lb. gorilla." Little wonder that the perceived value of the supplier to its dealers is negligible, and that the dealers seek every opportunity to carry alternative brands. Another manufacturer of equipment for the plastics industry took its product to market through independent sales agencies. Recognizing the crucial role these sales agencies played in delivering superior value to end users, this manufacturer included representatives from key agencies in its planning initiatives. By making the value creation and delivery processes transparent throughout the entire channel of distribution, this manufacturer was able to double its market share in targeted markets within a single year, while simultaneously making dramatic increases to its bottom line.

The decision to include channel members in the competitive market planning process requires a shift from a technological perspective on value to a customer or market perspective. Retaining a technological perspective is like trying to fight the competitive value war with one hand tied behind your back. For more on value-driven channel strategies, see Reidenbach and Goeke (2005).

## 10. Integrate the Discipline of Other Initiatives

Most organizations already have a number of quality or other training initiatives in place. Integrating those into the overall customer value management initiative will typically result in a "whole that is greater than the sum of its parts." The disciplines of Six Sigma and lean thinking, the perspective from value engineering, or the tools of Quality Function Deployment (QFD) can all contribute immeasurably to the successful deployment of your organization's customer value management system.

The discipline that the tools of Six Sigma provide can be especially valuable to the deployment of a successful competitive planning system. Six Sigma is as much a philosophy as it is a set of tools, and that philosophy of benchmarking and tracking performance with the appropriate metrics is precisely the sort of discipline required for the successful deployment of customer value. Conversely, the tools of customer value can transform the traditional Six Sigma perspective from a focus on cost reduction to a more strategic focus on revenue enhancement. The customer value quality drivers are precisely those critical-to-quality factors (CTQs) that are intended to drive specific Six Sigma projects. Linking the metrics of customer value to the metrics of Six Sigma means that future Six Sigma projects will have the strategic utility of enhancing performance on the most important CTQ factor. (For a more detailed description of this linkage, and the tools required to make it happen, see Reidenbach and Goeke, 2006).

Caterpillar is one of many major corporations to make a substantial commitment to the deployment of Six Sigma. One of Caterpillar's dealers recognized the potential benefits of integrating the discipline of Six Sigma with the strategic thrust of customer value, and appointed a Six Sigma Black Belt to each of its competitive market planning teams, with remarkable results. The Black Belts were quick to recognize and apply the appropriate metrics for tracking progress toward the attainment of plan objectives, bringing a rigor to plan performance reviews that had previously been lacking. But, equally important, the organization's Black Belts and Master Black Belts were quick to see that the systematic development of a competitive marketing plan based on CTQ factors would lead inexorably to the identification of the most important Six Sigma projects. The step-by-step linkage

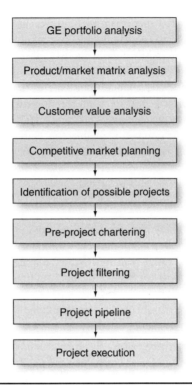

**Figure 11.1**   Customer value linkage to Six Sigma.

from customer value management to Six Sigma is illustrated in Figure 11.1. Each of the first five steps in this linkage has been described in this book. The last four steps will be familiar to any Six Sigma Black Belt, culminating with the execution of DMAIC.

This integration of customer value and quality initiatives not only provides a more strategic direction for Six Sigma, but also brings cohesiveness to the organization's future direction. This cohesiveness contributes significantly to a successful deployment by making it clear that the organization is not moving forward in several *different* directions.

## 11. Plan Performance Reviews

One of the most important keys to both short-term and long-term success is the routine scheduling of periodic plan performance reviews. This is important for short-term success just to ensure that plan implementation gets off to a good running start. But it's even more important for long-term success to ensure that the plan becomes a "living, dynamic plan," rather than simply a static set of objectives that, once achieved, are "finished."

We recommend scheduling plan performance reviews on a monthly basis, at least for the first year of implementation. One month seems to be the appropriate horizon for keeping each manager's attention fully focused on effective deployment. The first two or three performance reviews may take as long as a half day, as team members come to interpret and clarify the performance measures associated with each targeted action. Subsequent reviews will typically be completed within two hours.

Most plans will have a finite set of marketing mix objectives and actions that must be completed before additional objectives can be set. Benchmarking employee skill levels, for example, may be required prior to designing additional training programs. Monthly performance reviews will ensure that short-term objectives are met, and that additional . . . longer-term objectives are set. Additionally, plan performance reviews may reveal that the marketing mix objectives previously identified are insufficient to fully capitalize on the market value opportunities with which they are associated. Monthly reviews will help ensure that the plan grows to fulfill the intended strategy.

## 12. Evaluate Alignment of Corporate, Business-Unit, and Product/Market Strategies

The three different levels and purposes of planning were discussed in the very first Chapter of this book. To recap, the purpose of corporate planning is for overall growth, the purpose of business-unit planning is for strategic focus, and the purpose of product/market planning is for sustainable competitive advantage. The outcomes from each planning level should be reviewed on a periodic basis to be sure that all three levels remain in alignment.

Suppose, for example, that the overall emphasis for corporate growth was to shift from a focus on market penetration to a focus on product development, or to a focus on market development. What would be the implications for the business-unit plan? Would the business unit continue to invest resources in the targeted product/markets, as determined by a market penetration strategy? What would be the implications for the development of each business unit's product/market matrix?

Or, suppose that the business unit manager reevaluated the product/market matrix based on updated information, and concluded that additional resources should be devoted to a product/market previously considered to be relatively unimportant. What happens if those resources are pulled from the current planning team and redirected to the new product/market?

This alignment of strategies may seem too obvious to explicitly raise as a key to the long-term success of deployment. But we are struck by how frequently one level or another within the organization will shift strategies without considering the consequences for the strategies at other levels of the organization. One senior management team had long focused on market penetration and market development as the keys to corporate growth. As new markets were developed, new business units were created, each with the explicit objective of increasing market share within targeted product/markets. As the current markets became saturated and new markets were increasingly harder to identify, the senior management team concluded that product development would need to become a key to the corporate growth strategy. Rather than developing that strategy at the corporate level, however, the corporate executives placed that challenge at the feet of its business-unit managers, producing total confusion at the business-unit level. Those business-unit executives continued to feel the pressure of maintaining market share in the face of more intense competition, but were constantly distracted by the need to "find some new product" that might fit into the organization's overall portfolio. The result, of course, was that neither product development nor market penetration succeeded as strategies for corporate growth.

## 13. Structure Follows Strategy

One serious impediment to the successful deployment of a competitive planning system is management's penchant for structural change. It would seem that business schools are doing a remarkably good job of convincing managers that they can always have a substantial impact on an organization if they'll just tweak the organizational structure a bit. We have seen many instances when the deployment of a customer value management system seemed to be successfully underway, only to grind to a complete stop because senior management decided to restructure the organization. Such restructuring can move key people to other areas of the organization, and frequently causes progress of any sort to stop simply due to the anxiety created by the restructuring.

We are not arguing that there is never a need for restructuring. We do take the position, however, that an organization's structure must be designed to support the organization's strategy, not the other way around. If there is no clear, overarching strategy, no amount of restructuring will improve business performance. If, however, the organization is committed to winning customers by providing superior value, then the organization's structure must be designed to support that strategy.

One international company, identified by the American Productivity and Quality Center as a "Best Practice" company, has developed such a structure in support of its strategy "to be the outstanding provider of value in those products and markets in which we choose to compete." That structure is depicted in Figure 11.2.

Historically, this organization was structured around its key functional areas: new equipment sales, used equipment sales, rentals, parts, and service. Each of these functional areas functioned as a business unit, with market share and profitability objectives. As the organization evolved into one focused on the creation and delivery of superior value, its managers realized that the existing structure could not support the intended strategy. Salespeople in the "New Equipment Sales" department were competing with used equipment and rentals for the customers' business, and none of them were particularly interested in selling the smaller equipment for smaller commissions. Customers had no single point of contact for equipment repairs. Each

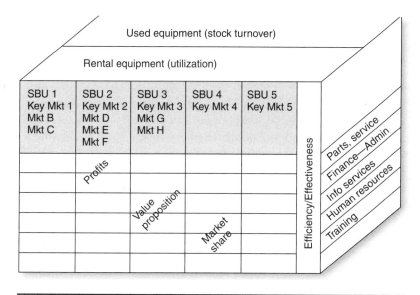

**Figure 11.2**   A structure in support of a strategy.

division was focused on its products; none was focused on specific groups of customers. This was clearly not a structure that could support a focus on customer value.

The restructuring of this organization, as shown in Figure 11.2, provides the appropriate customer focus. Each business unit, identified as SBU 1 through 5, is focused on a strategically important market as determined by the organization's portfolio analysis. Markets that are less strategically important are distributed among the five business units to be sure that those markets are still served without drawing down strategic resources. Within each business unit, a product/market matrix identified two product lines for strategic focus, resulting in a focus on two key product/markets for each business unit. Business-unit performance is evaluated on three key criteria: its competitive value propositions in the priority product/market (40 percent), market share (30 percent), and profitability (30 percent). The rationale for the evaluative weightings is that profitable market share will follow a winning value proposition, and the latter is what can be most effectively managed.

The functional support areas of the company, parts, service, information systems, HR, and so forth operate in support of the five business units. Each supporting manager is responsible to the business-unit manager for maximizing both the effectiveness and the efficiency of that support. "Effectiveness" is a function of performance on key quality drivers for each targeted product/market within each business unit. "Efficiency" is evaluated in terms of low cost, without creating a negative impact on key quality drivers. Both are typically driven by Six Sigma initiatives. The used equipment area is still managed separately due to its international ramifications, and the rental area is similarly managed, but both areas report through the five business units to ensure that customers don't receive conflicting messages.

Embarking on competitive planning deployment does *not* necessarily mean that you should immediately begin considering restructuring, no matter what your current structure. In fact, our experience suggests that any attempt to restructure in the early stages of deployment would likely be counterproductive. As you look to long-term success, however, be sure to evaluate whether your current structure provides adequate support for the new strategy. Don't be surprised if your competitive planning system does not push you toward a different structure, one centered around the market.

## 14. Manage Culture Change

Shifting from a product focus to a market focus, or from a technological focus to a customer and competitor focus, involves a significant change to the culture of an organization. In our experience, this is a particularly positive change, but it must nevertheless be managed.

Organizations that have embarked on Six Sigma or lean journeys typically report that those initiatives also entail a significant culture change. The change experienced by those companies is frequently characterized as a change from management by intuition to management by facts, from a relatively undisciplined culture to a culture disciplined by objective data and definitive metrics. Employees involved in the transition are often shocked by the efficiencies that can be attained and the cost reductions in operations that can be achieved. Once those efficiencies are documented, they engender even more enthusiasm for further efficiencies and cost reductions until, ultimately, the entire organization is on fire with a zeal for speed and zero defects. This transition is most effectively managed with a disciplined documentation of process improvements.

The culture change experienced by an organization deploying a competitive planning system parallels some of the change experienced by Six Sigma and lean organizations. That is, competitive planning is also characterized as a shift from management by intuition to management by fact and toward a far more disciplined planning and management style. But the culture change in a market-driven organization also entails shifting from an internal perspective to an external perspective, from a product orientation to a market orientation. And this transition of cultures must also be carefully managed. Employees throughout the organization must understand *why* the organization is shifting its focus exclusively from cost containment to value enhancement. They must understand why and how management has determined that some customers are simply more important to the organization than others, but that this setting of priorities does *not* mean that the organization will *stop serving all customers*. And they must understand precisely what it is that drives value for their targeted customers, and what their role is in delivering that value.

Managers must have an especially strong set of leadership skills to effect this culture change, because it is not one that happens quickly. Managers should become immersed in the tools of customer value so they can clearly articulate what it is that's driving the organization's competitive strategies, what the targeted value proposition is for each strategy, and how their own functional areas will be contributing to the attainment of that target. Managers must also be prepared to counter "prevailing intuition" with objective facts, and should strive to fully document all process improvements and their results.

The successful deployment of a competitive planning system based on value is an extremely exciting and rewarding endeavor. Aligning internal and external mental models of value is the first and most important step toward successful deployment. Demonstrating the systematic nature of developing a value-based, market-driven competitive plan to your management team will be the next big step in transforming the organization. Linking the voice of customer value to process improvements through lean, Six Sigma, and other initiatives brings the deployment right down to the level of front-line employees. And monitoring progress toward value leadership is particularly exciting when followed by profitable increases in market share. Enjoy the journey!

# 12

# Competing for Customers

Competing successfully requires a systematic approach to the market-place. It begins with a choice as to which markets the organization wishes to target with·which products, and concludes with a monitoring system to make sure that the organization's competitive efforts are on target. In between is a logical and highly disciplined process for designing competitive strategies for value leadership. Sustainable value leadership translates into market leadership.

Figure 12.1 repeats the planning system first discussed in Chapter 1. This system consists of three planning levels, each charged with a different planning task. At the corporate level the task is to identify how the organization will grow. Four options for growth have been identified in Figure 12.1, and were described in Chapter 1.

At the SBU level the task is to determine where the organization will focus its competitive efforts and its limited resources. This is extremely important because most organizations are faced with a myriad set of opportunities, some of which are better than others. The identification of strategic priorities within each business unit is the single most important planning activity of business-unit managers, and requires the compilation of data pertaining to the chosen decision criteria within a product/market matrix, as described in Chapter 5. It is at this level where the organization becomes focused in its competitive efforts. And with this focus comes a power and intensity that makes competitive strategies stronger, more effective, and more efficient.

The product/markets selected for strategic focus are the competitive arenas in which the organization·unleashes its competitive efforts on a systematic basis. We emphasize "systematic" because these competitive initiatives must not be random, nor intuitive, nor merely reactive. Rather, the organization must understand the full breadth and depth of what drives value in each competitive arena better than any competitor, and must systematically apply that knowledge to the development and deployment of objectives

Corporate level: How does the organization grow?

SBU level: Where does the organization choose to compete?

P/M level: How does the organization compete?

What is the organization's current value proposition?
• What are the key value drivers?
• What are the firm's strengths and weaknesses?
• How does the firm stack up against competition?
• What are the firm's opportunities?

What is the firm's intended value proposition?
• What are the firm's performance objectives?
• What is the firm's strategy?
• What are the assumptions underlying the strategy?

How does the firm achieve its intended value proposition?
• What is the firm's marketing mix?
• What are the specific action plans?
• What are the action plan timelines?
• Who is responsible for actions?
• How do we know actions are accomplished?
• What are the direct costs of the actions?
• What are the forecasted results?

Has the firm achieved its objectives?

**Figure 12.1**   The context of competitive planning.

and strategies for a sustainable competitive advantage. It is the voice of the market that drives the organization's competitive efforts, not the voice of internal "experts" who can talk louder, or who have been bestowed with some mythical power based on their seniority.

## WHAT IS THE ORGANIZATION'S CURRENT VALUE PROPOSITION?

Competitive planning begins with answering the question "What is the organization's competitive value proposition within each of the product/markets it has targeted?" The answer to this question requires the organization for each product/market to:

- Understand how the targeted market defines value pertaining to the selected product

- Understand how the organization's competitive value proposition stands up to its competitors
  - What are the organization's strengths and weaknesses on
    - Value drivers
    - Quality drivers
    - Value performance criteria

- Understand what its opportunities for enhancing value are

## WHAT IS THE ORGANIZATION'S INTENDED VALUE PROPOSITION?

What happens when the organization's competitive value proposition is not what it wants? This happens all the time. In some organizations the value proposition is better than managers think it is, whereas in others, it is worse. In either case, the organization must delineate an intended value proposition that achieves its objectives. This requires:

- Identifying the organization's performance objectives. Performance objectives are of two kinds:
  - Market share or profitability objectives
  - Value objectives

- Articulate a strategy as a:
  - Leader
  - Challenger
  - Follower
  - Nicher

- Identify the assumptions underlying the strategy. These include factors such as:
  - Competitive trends
  - Sociocultural trends
  - Economic trends
  - Technological trends
  - Political/legal trends
  - Other trends that can affect the successful deployment of the firm's strategy

## How Does the Organization Achieve Its Intended Value Proposition?

This is the third critical question. To answer it the organization must be able to answer the following questions:

- What combination of product, price, promotion, and distribution are needed?

- What are the specific action plans?

- When will these individual actions be accomplished and by whom?

- How does the planning team know that the actions have been completed?

- What are the individual direct costs of each action?

- What are the forecasted results of each action?

The answers to these questions provide the impetus for achieving the organization's intended value proposition. They provide a step-by-step plan for achieving the organization's strategy identified earlier.

One organization, in support of its value strategy and emanating from its action plans, developed a value-based sales program. Training programs were developed in conjunction with sales managers based on the key value drivers. Supporting this approach was the information taken from the competitor vulnerability matrix, in which competitors' customers were profiled on their evaluations of their current suppliers, performance on the value drivers. When customers came into the dealership, salespeople would probe regarding their current supplier and knew what their strengths and weaknesses were and could address the advantages their product provided over that of their competition. In this way they were speaking directly to what the customer valued and what the customer was not getting in his or her current relationship. This included not only product but also other aspects of the value equation such as product support, product training, parts, and so on.

# HAS THE ORGANIZATION
# ACHIEVED ITS OBJECTIVES?

Too often organizations fail to monitor progress toward their objectives. Once the competitive plan is crafted and deployed, it has been our experience that many organizations fail to determine whether the plan is doing what it is intended to do. At this point, many managers frequently resort once again to the exclusive use of internal metrics to monitor progress. These might include the monitoring of response times, turnaround time on repairs, or a host of internal financial metrics. Although internal metrics are useful for a numbers of reasons, the real measure of effectiveness is what customers can actually see and feel. This requires the development of a measurement system that can quantify the organization's progress toward the intended value proposition, and to identify any aberrations along the way. The old adage about not being able to manage what you can't measure applies here. The true test of an evolving value proposition will be market based, but every organization requires periodic monitoring of transactions from a customer perspective, as described in Chapter 10.

Like all wars, individual battles are won in the trenches, not at headquarters. In this case the trenches are the specific product/markets that the organization targets for competition. The battle is won by selling more tractors, brokerage accounts, cars, computers, or cheese than the competition. To do this the organization must be able to create and deliver greater value than its competitors. In the competition for customers it is the organization that can out-value its competitors that will win in the end.

# Appendix A

## Technical Notes on Value Measurement

### ATTRIBUTES/VALUE PERFORMANCE CRITERIA

The attributes discussed in this appendix are the individual questionnaire items used by customers to evaluate the performance of suppliers. The questions are performance-based questions that ask the respondent to rate a supplier based on how well the organization performs on the individual attributes. Because they are stated in such a way as to require a performance evaluation, we also refer to these attributes as *value performance criteria.*

It is important to note that the attributes elicit responses to the individual questionnaire items both from customers of your organization and from customers of your key competitors. Accordingly, the resulting model is a market-based model and not a client-specific model. One of the most salient characteristics of value is its relativity, which makes it a uniquely suited construct for competitive intelligence. The nature of competing for customers is characterized by its dynamism, and that dynamism requires a metric that enables comparisons of one competitive offering with another. The attributes themselves come from focus groups of current and potential users of the product or service under analysis and become the questionnaire items.

### IMPORTANCE SCORES: STATED VERSUS DERIVED

In addition to gathering performance measures, some organizations will also gather importance scores. This makes the questionnaire almost twice as long for the respondent and can cause a significant amount of respondent attrition and subsequent nonresponse. Moreover, frequently the performance scores and importance scores are correlated, causing a significant problem with the error terms and confounding the quality and meaning of the data. Using performance scores within a regression format allows the generation of *derived importance* scores such as those associated with each value and quality driver in the model. These derived importance scores are interpretable as the relative importance of each driver in explaining value, and accommodate the complex interactions that take place among the various quality, image, and price drivers that typical market research ignores.

Value is the interaction between the quality, image, and price of a product or service. The middle part of the model depicts this relationship. The numbers next to each component reflect the importance of each component in defining value. For example, the model shown in Figure 3.1 shows a quality component (CQI) that is about twice as important as either the image or price components. This importance is interpretable as a *strategic importance*. By that it is meant that the higher the score, the greater the overall variability among the competitors' quality components. If the score were small it would be indicating that all competitors were offering about the same level of quality. The greater the number, the greater the variability and the greater the opportunity to differentiate. Customers across the market are seeing a difference in the quality offerings of the various competitors. In the model shown in Figure 3.1, the proper interpretation of both the image and the price variable would be that there is significantly less opportunity to differentiate the organization's value proposition based on image and price. According to this model, customers do not see much difference among the competitors on these two factors.

This differentiation issue is particularly important with regard to price. In many industries too much emphasis has been placed on price, and companies have marketed themselves into a commodity-like situation where there is great fear in raising price. Models of this situation typically show a very low derived-importance weight for price. They reflect the market's understanding that all competitors are charging a similar price.

The numbers between the image component and the CQI and price indicate the strength of the relationship between the image factor and the quality and price components. This points out that changes in either the quality or price elements will also impact the organization's image.

# MULTICOLLINEARITY

There is a single arrow going from the collective nonprice drivers to the CQI. The CQI is the customer quality index, comprised of the individual quality drivers and weighted by their derived importance scores. The CQI represents a single quality factor. This is useful for one critically important reason. Using all the quality drivers along with the image driver and the price driver runs the risk of creating a situation called *multicollinearity*. Multicollinearity occurs when the independent variables (quality drivers, image, and price) are more highly correlated among themselves than with the dependent variable (value). The outcome of multicollinearity is a distortion of the derived importance weights such that they may be over-or understated and/or they may have negative signs attached to them. In either case, they cannot be trusted and their interpretation is certainly suspect.

# R SQUARES

The robustness or quality of the model is reflected in the $R^2$ score. This score ($R^2$) can vary between 0 and 1. The closer to 1, the more powerful is the model. And, while $R^2$s of 1 are not common, a good model should have a $R^2$ between .75 and .90.

# MODEL CHARACTERISTICS

As mentioned earlier, the value model is different from a market research report. This difference is manifest in several very important areas.

## Identifying Relationships

First, the model makes explicit the relationships among the various elements that comprise value. Just as a model airplane represents a real airplane and shows how a wing is attached to the fuselage or how a propeller or engine is attached to a wing, a well-developed value model reflects what specific customers using a specific product mean by *value* and how the different elements interact. The model permits the examination of the parts that comprise the model. For example, the model provides managers with the opportunity to play "what if" games. By changing an organization's scores on either the individual attributes or drivers, the resultant impact on value can be seen. Additionally, costs for these proposed changes can be estimated to see if the return on value is worth it. This can't be done with the standard market research report.

## Multiple Measures

Second, the model is developed with multiple measures. This is important because the reliability and the validity of the model can only be assessed when multiple measures are used. Most market research does not provide evidence of reliability because most market research does not include multiple measures of individual constructs. This leads to the likelihood that different respondents may "mean" different things when responding to a single measure. What does a respondent mean when he or she gives a score of 7 (on a 10-point scale) to a question about the organization's responsiveness? What is the respondent telling you? What does *responsive* mean? Does it mean the same thing for all respondents? The problem is that no one knows the answers to these questions. How do you formulate a competitive plan to become organizationally more responsive if you are not sure about what the market means by *responsive*? Multiple measures of "responsiveness" (time taken to answer phone, response time for product information request, speed of responding on-site for a service call and so forth) not only provide clearer direction for effective competitive planning, but also allow for the statistical calculation of reliability—something that cannot be done without multiple measures.

If measures aren't reliable, they cannot be valid. This is a related issue. Let's say you are measuring satisfaction. How do you know that you are actually measuring satisfaction? Does the mere mention of the word ensure that you are in fact measuring satisfaction? What about value? Are you really measuring value or something else? The issue of validity is critical. In the physical world, scales can be calibrated, time synchronized, distances measured, and so on. But this is not so in consumer research. Multiple measures go a long way toward addressing the strategically important issues of reliability and validity. Formulating a competitive plan from competitive information that is not demonstrably valid is akin to guessing. The quality of the plan is a direct function of whether you have actual and valid measures of either satisfaction or value. If not, any success from plan development and deployment is simply a random occurrence. The lack of valid measures will sabotage even the most elaborate planning and execution.

Typical market research pays little, if any, attention to issues of reliability and validity. The information provided in most market research is questionable and not the stuff on which sound competitive planning should be based. Little wonder that many business managers are reluctant to develop competitive plans on the basis of their existing market research. Without evidence of the reliability and validity of the competitive intelligence, many managers feel more secure with their own intuition!

## Market-Based Models

Third, the value model is a market-based model derived from customers who use your product or service and those who use competitors' products and services. Market-based models are essential because it is through them that the dynamics of gaining and losing customers is captured. Models or data reflecting only your customers cannot capture this dynamism and cannot inform the competitive planning process. The competitive value model is the basis for the other three value tools.

# Appendix B

## Environmental Trend Analysis

Every company and its suppliers, competitors, customers, and intermediaries operates in a macroenvironment of trends and forces that shape its opportunities and pose threats to future business success. Many organizations have a formal process for codifying those trends. Others evaluate trends on a more informal basis.

Environmental trend analysis is a critical component of an effective competitive market planning process. Planning teams must be mindful of trends affecting the organization as a whole, but should be particularly attentive to trends that may provide opportunities or create threats associated with their competitive plan at the product/market level. This is not an exercise that should be conducted annually, but one that should be ongoing and reviewed, if briefly, at monthly plan performance reviews. The collection of data pertaining to environmental trends can now be automated using such simple tools as a Google, Yahoo, or an MSN search engine. These and other Internet search engines are quite capable of providing daily, weekly, or monthly alerts pertaining to key words or phrases provided. Selecting and refining those key words over time will yield a treasure trove of useful information on a routine basis.

Beyond simply collecting data that may help to document a trend, environmental trend analysis consists of thoughtful reflection regarding what specific trends may mean to a business or, in this case, to the effectiveness of a competitive marketing plan. Trends pertaining to economic developments, social or cultural evolutions that may lead to political and legal action, new technologies, or competitive trends that are beyond your organization's control could all pose a threat to your competitive marketing plan or, indeed, may lead to an opportunity. The community reacting negatively to construction noise may lead to legislation regulating operating hours or acceptable sound levels. The regulation of construction operating hours may negatively impact the market growth rate, with implications for projected unit sales. The regulation of acceptable sound levels could present a genuine opportunity if your product development activity has anticipated this regulation and you are the only provider to meet the new standards.

In any event, data must be routinely collected and analyzed to identify any potential trends in the macroenvironment. These trends should then be documented, evaluated to determine what impact, if any, they may have on the effectiveness of your competitive marketing plan, and when that impact is likely to occur. An example of such an analysis pertaining to skid steer loaders for the building construction business is provided in the accompanying chart.

In addition to using this analysis for the identification of potential threats or opportunities, it will lead to the identification of specific assumptions upon which the plan is based. Constant monitoring of the trends underlying those assumptions will become a critical part of plan performance reviews.

| Major trend to affect business | Date of impact | Consequences | Evidence |
|---|---|---|---|
| Economic: | | | |
| • Has been high growth. Expected to continue for several more years, but at a lower rate. | Began 3 years ago and continuing | Continuing increase in Skid Steer sales. Must do better job of forecasting growth in order to have correct inventory levels. | Replacement cycle, about 10–12K hours. Much more turnover in SS than in HEX. Increasing interest rates. |
| • Commodities (building materials) increasing in price. | | Will begin to slow growth. | Last 3 years of NCSA records. |
| Competition: | | | |
| • Competitors (esp. @ Competitor 3) getting better at product support; investing in this area. | Current | Diminishing impact of a traditional [Company XYZ] strength. | Performance rating through CVA. |
| • New brands/suppliers entering the market. | Last 2 years and continuing | Most of the new players in lower price/quality range. Not impacting our sales just yet, but may. | [Brand XYZ] in last 4 years. Also Komatsu Hyundai, Daewoo, Volvo, ASV, Takeuchi, Cougar— more recently. |
| • Movement toward greater utilization of work tools. Multiple applications. | | Must assure availability. May need alternate suppliers. | |
| • Increasing factory-supported floor planning. | Last 6 months and continuing | Competitors will have stock available for trial/loan. | Must quantify (esp. Toyota, Bobcat). |

*(continued)*

| Major trend to affect business | Date of impact | Consequences | Evidence |
|---|---|---|---|
| Technology:<br>• Easy accessibility—international access via Internet. | Within next 12–24 months | Increased availability of low-hour used equipment.<br>Transparency of pricing. | Easy international access to equipment, esp. through Internet. |
| Political/Legal:<br>• Movement toward more rigorous emissions controls. | 2006 and beyond | Possible negative impact on Sumitomo, Daewoo, and Hyundai because they don't currently have anything in place. | Document. |
| • More stringent controls concerning disposal of waste products/fluids. | 2006 | Increased costs may push responsibility back from owners to dealers. | Must investigate differences internationally. |
| • Increasing concern about safety. | 2007 | ROPS/FOPS implications. | Pending legislation. |
| • Need for operator certification. | 2005 | Engineering complications.<br>With introduction of new products, increased need for training. | Passage of legislation in certain parts of the country. |
| Sociocultural:<br>• Increasing pressure to lower noise levels. | 2006 | Restriction of operating hours. | Increased regulations and increased community knowledge on their rights. |

# Appendix C

## Competitive Market Planning Forms

# Insert Product/Market:

# Customer Value Management Strategy Development Team

## Insert Team Members:

## Strategic Management Plan Insert Date:

# PRODUCT/MARKET MATRIX

**Note:** The product/market matrix should be constructed for each business unit within the organization. Markets, or market segments, are listed across the top; product lines are listed down the left side. Select criteria for the evaluation of product/market cells, then enter data pertaining to those criteria into each cell. List the criteria as the "Key." Include totals for the rows and the columns. Rank order the priorities. Identify the product/market that will be the focus of this plan.

SBU: _____

Date: _____

| *Market* **Product** | | | | | | | | | | **Total** |
|---|---|---|---|---|---|---|---|---|---|---|
| | | | | | | | | | | |
| | | | | | | | | | | |
| | | | | | | | | | | |
| | | | | | | | | | | |
| | | | | | | | | | | |
| | | | | | | | | | | |
| | | | | | | | | | | |
| **Total** | | | | | | | | | | |

KEY:

# ENVIRONMENTAL SCANNING

**Note:** The purpose of scanning is to identify those trends that will have an impact on the market's definition of value and impact either your organization's competitive value proposition or that of its competition. Environmental trends are beyond the organization's capacity to control. Consequently, your company must react to them. Obviously, by anticipating these trends and their impacts on your competitive value proposition, your organization is in a better position to proactively deal with them as opposed to reactively dealing with them.

| Major trend to affect business | Date of impact | Consequences | Evidence |
|---|---|---|---|
| Economic:<br><br>• | | | |
| Competition:<br><br>• | | | |
| Technology:<br><br>• | | | |
| Political/Legal:<br><br>• | | | |
| Sociocultural:<br><br>• | | | |

# QUALIFYING NEEDS OF SEGMENT

**Note:** Qualifiers are one of two kinds of customer needs. Organizations refer to "qualifying needs" by such phrases as "must haves," "table stakes," or "antes." Their role in the purchase process is extremely important. Failure to "qualify" has several consequences. In some cases failure to qualify closes an organization out of a market. In other cases it may mean that the organization can only do business in a reduced portion of the market.

The purpose of identifying qualifiers is to assess the organization's capacity to satisfy them, thus allowing the organization to get into the game. Candidate qualifiers often are identified as those factors that do not load in the value model. In addition, the planning team, because of their experience with the segment, is also a good source of potential qualifiers.

# DETERMINING NEEDS OF SEGMENT

**Note:** The second type of customer need is the determiner, or driver. These needs are important because the organization's capacity to perform well on these needs wins the game. The needs identified here come from the customer value analysis and are the drivers identified within the value model. Some drivers are more important than others. The importance of the drivers is indicated in the "Relative Contribution to Value Proposition" column.

| Determining need | Relative contribution to value proposition |
|---|---|
| **Customer Quality Index** | |
| [Driver] | |
| [Driver] | |
| [Driver] | |
| [Driver] | |
| **PRICE** | |

# MARKET SHARE AND TRENDS

**Note:** List each key competitor from the competitive value matrix. Document or estimate sales and market share for the previous year. Indicate whether the market share trend over the last three years has been up, down, or flat. Identify the value position from the competitive value matrix. Indicate whether the value position has been improving, declining, or stable.

| Competitor | Unit sales | Dollar sales (000) | Market share (%) | Trend | Value position | Trend |
|---|---|---|---|---|---|---|
|  |  |  |  |  |  |  |
|  |  |  |  |  |  |  |
|  |  |  |  |  |  |  |
|  |  |  |  |  |  |  |
|  |  |  |  |  |  |  |
|  |  |  |  |  |  |  |
|  |  |  |  |  |  |  |
|  |  |  |  |  |  |  |
| TOTAL |  |  |  |  |  |  |

# VALUE PROPOSITION ASSESSMENT

**Note:** Transfer competitive value propositions for your company and each competitor from the customer value analysis.

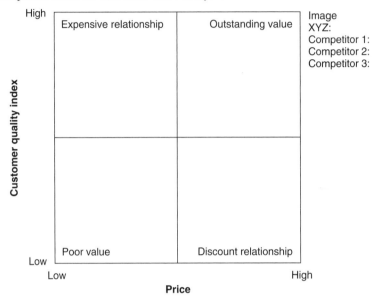

## DIFFERENTIAL VALUE ADVANTAGE/DISADVANTAGE

| P/M: | Co 1 | Co 2 | Co 3 | Co 4 | Co 5 | Co 6 | Co 7 |
|---|---|---|---|---|---|---|---|
| | Mean | Mean | Mean | Mean | Mean | Mean | Mean |
| CQI | | | | | | | |
| - [Driver 1] | | | | | | | |
| - [Driver 2] | | | | | | | |
| - [Driver 3] | | | | | | | |
| - [Driver . . . n] | | | | | | | |
| Pricing | | | | | | | |
| Image | | | | | | | |

Competitive advantage     Competitive disadvantage

# MARKET OPPORTUNITY IDENTIFICATION

**Note:** Market opportunities are derived from the matching of an organization's strengths and weaknesses with the qualifying and determining needs (drivers) of the segment. The first place an organization should look for opportunities is if they have any weaknesses on qualifiers. Failure to qualify means that the organization is either completely foreclosed from competing effectively within a segment or is partially foreclosed. The second place to look for market opportunities is if the organization has any strengths on important value drivers, or parity positions that could be turned into strengths. It is our experience that organizations get greater marketing returns by leveraging strengths than addressing weaknesses. Exceptions to this might include weaknesses on important drivers. Hence, the third source of opportunities comes from organizational weaknesses on important drivers.

| Strengths: | | | |
|---|---|---|---|
| Value driver: | | | |
| Other: | | | |
| **Weaknesses:** | | | |
| Qualifier: | | | |
| Value driver: | | | |
| Other: | | | |
| **Market opportunities:** | | | |

# STRATEGY AND OBJECTIVES

**Note:** There are essentially four strategic options facing any organization. These options are dependent upon the organization's competitive value proposition and its market share position. Organizations can choose to *lead, challenge, follow,* or *niche.* The choice of a specific option is followed by those opportunities that will ensure the organization's achievement of the product/market objectives. This comprises the product/market strategy statement.

| | |
|---|---|
| P/M objectives: <br><br> • | |
| Product market strategy: | |
| **Objectives** | |
| Opportunity 1: <br><br> 1.1 Objective 1 for opportunity 1. <br> 1.2 Objective 2 for opportunity 1. | |

# PRODUCT/MARKET ACTION PROGRAMS

**Note:** For every objective identified within specific opportunities there will be one or more actions necessary to reach that objective. Each action must be accompanied by an associated milestone indicating when the action is to be completed, a performance measure indicating when it is completed, a responsibility designation (one person), and a direct cost estimate.

| Actions | Key milestone | Performance measures | Responsibility | Cost |
|---------|---------------|----------------------|----------------|------|
|         |               |                      |                |      |
|         |               |                      |                |      |
|         |               |                      |                |      |
|         |               |                      |                |      |
|         |               |                      |                |      |
|         |               |                      |                |      |
|         |               |                      |                |      |
|         |               |                      |                |      |

# BUDGET AND MARKET FORECAST

**Note:** Transfer costs from the cost column of the action programs. Be sure to identify them with the appropriate time frame. Calculate incremental revenue, less cost of goods sold, based on the product/market objectives. Where possible, include ancillary incremental revenues, such as those attributable to incremental support revenue. Subtract costs from revenues to identify plan contribution for each period.

| Cost category | Last year | This year | | | | Year 1 | Year 2 | Year 3 | Year 4 | Year 5 |
|---|---|---|---|---|---|---|---|---|---|---|
| | | Q1 | Q2 | Q3 | Q4 | | | | | |
| Sales expense | | | | | | | | | | |
| Service expense | | | | | | | | | | |
| Marketing expense | | | | | | | | | | |
| Other direct expense | | | | | | | | | | |
| Total expense | | | | | | | | | | |

| Contributions | Last year | This year | | | | Year 1 | Year 2 | Year 3 | Year 4 | Year 5 |
|---|---|---|---|---|---|---|---|---|---|---|
| | | Q1 | Q2 | Q3 | Q4 | | | | | |
| Plan revenue | | | | | | | | | | |
| Plan contribution | | | | | | | | | | |

# Glossary

**attributes**—Questionnaire items used to measure performance. Also referred to as *value performance criteria*. When sorted into groups using a factor analytic process, these attributes become part of a potential value drive (factor).

**competitive value matrix**—The competitive value matrix identifies the competitive value propositions of the various competitors. It does so by juxtaposing the customer quality index with the price driver. Organizations' CQI and price scores are used to locate the organization within the matrix space.

**competitive value proposition**—An organization's competitive value proposition is identified on the competitive value matrix and is formed by the intersection of the CQI and price coordinates. It is a signal to the market regarding the level of value customers can expect from any individual supplier.

**CRM**—CRM (customer relationship management) is a tool that is based on information compiled about individual customers. Its purpose is to provide the organization with information that enables it to measure and track the economic value of the customer to the organization.

**customer quality index**—The customer quality index (CQI) is a weighted index of the various quality drivers that comprise it. It is an aggregated measure of quality that includes elements of product, service, and channel.

**CVA/CVM**—CVA (customer value analysis) is the measurement component of CVM (customer value management). CVM encompasses not only CVA but also planning and continuous improvement components.

**driver**—There are two types of drivers—value drivers and quality drivers. Value drivers consist of the customer quality index (CQI), image, and price. The quality drivers are those factors that comprise the CQI.

**driver reliability score**—Reliability is a necessary but insufficient condition for validity. Driver reliability, usually measured by a coefficient alpha ($\alpha$), indicates the degree to which the attributes that comprise a driver measure a similar concept. Coefficient alphas range between zero and one. The higher the a, the more reliable the measure.

**driver weight**—Identifies the relative impact of individual drivers. The driver weight is often referred to as the "derived importance" of a driver and is represented by a beta weight.

**factor analysis**—An analytic procedure used for sorting attributes into linear combinations called factors. These factors represent latent dimensions in that they provide a richer understanding of purchase criteria. Factor analysis is used to reduce the set of value performance criteria (attributes) into a smaller set of more robust criteria.

**image**—New to most value configurations, image can play an important role in value depending on which industry you are in. Image has a reciprocal relationship with the other value drivers; it affects performance perceptions of them while at the same time image is affected by how a firm performs on those drivers.

**loyalty**—*Attitudinal loyalty* is typically measured by "willingness to recommend" or "willingness to switch" under varying price discounts. It captures a customer's intention. *Behavioral loyalty* is the customer's demonstrated willingness to repurchase a product or service or renew a contract. It is the true measure of loyalty.

**market segment**—A group of customers who have similar needs and similar definitions of value. A market may be comprised of various individual segments.

**market value opportunity**—A market-defined opportunity for an organization to achieve sustainable value differentiation. Market value opportunities are based upon correcting market-perceived weaknesses and/or leveraging market-perceived strengths on key value drivers.

**model fit**—Measures the robustness or power of the model to explain value and/or loyalty. Model fit is typically measured as $R^2$. which ranges between 0 (no fit) and 1 (perfect fit). Fits of greater than 0.70 should be targeted.

**multicollinearity**—Multicollinearity is a condition in which the independent variables have a greater degree of association among them than does an independent variable with a dependent variable.

**price satisfaction**—The value model and other value tools rely on evaluations of competitors' pricing policies. Price satisfaction rates individual pricing points in terms of their fairness and competitiveness.

**product line**—A group of similar products as judged by customers. Products within a product line may be substitutable while products between product lines are less substitutable.

**product/market**—A specific market segment that uses a specific product or product line. A product/market combines the two elements of revenue production, and products and customers, and in so doing provides a finer focal point for measurement, planning, and process improvement. Product/markets are identified in the product/market matrix.

**qualifying dimension**—A "must have," "table stakes" or "entry into the game." A dimension characterized by a low-quality weighting or a low-value weighting and low variability. Poor performance on a qualifying dimension can seriously impede an organization's ability to compete within a product/market.

**regression analysis**—A statistical technique used to assess the degree of association between a set of independent variables and a dependent variable. The degree of association is expressed in the $R^2$ statistic, which can vary between 0 (no association) and 1 (perfect association). In modeling, the higher the $R^2$, the better the model fit.

**strategic criteria**—Strategic criteria include such elements as gross margin, market share, market growth rates, competitive intensity, and other measures used to evaluate and prioritize the opportunities within a product/market matrix.

**value**—While individuals are involved in decisions regarding different products and services, the nature and mechanics of their decisions are not dissimilar. In making a choice of a particular supplier, all individuals are asking a fundamental question. "If I chose Company X's product/service, will it be worth it?" At the very heart of the "worth it" question is the issue of value.

**value proposition**—*Existing value proposition*—How the market views and interprets your value offering. Your organization's value proposition interpreted relative to that of your competition. *Intended value proposition*—How you want the market to interpret your organization's value offering.

**value stream**—A set of processes, functions, and activities that are involved in the actual delivery of value to a product/market. The value stream is the focal point for significant targeted improvement efforts for enhancing an organization's competitive value proposition.

**value stream analysis (VSA)**—An analytical process designed to (1) enhance the benefit(s) of a value delivery system while (2) reducing or eliminating all non-value-adding costs associated with value delivery.

**vulnerability matrix**—The vulnerability matrix identifies the degree of loyalty of competitors' customers and the basis of that loyalty. This is an important tool in the acquisition of competitors' customers.

# References

Ansoff, I. 1957. 'Strategies for diversification,' *Harvard Business Review* (Sept.–Oct.), pp. 113–124.

American Productivity and Quality Center. 2002. *Leveraging customer value to drive business performance.*

B2B ain't what it used to be. 2005. *eMarketer Report,* eMarketer, Inc.

Buchanan, R., and C. Gilles. 1990. Value managed relationship: The key to customer retention and profitability. *European Management Journal,* V. 8, No. 4.

Gale, B. 1994. *Managing customer value.* New York: The Free Press.

McConnell, B., and J. Huba. 2002. Creating customer evangelists: how loyal customers become a volunteer sales force. *Dearborn Trade* (December).

Morgan, N. A., E. W. Anderson, and V. Mittal. 2005. *Understanding firms customer satisfaction information usage. Journal of Marketing* (July), pp. 131–151.

Porter, M. 1985. *Competitive advantage: creating and sustaining superior performance.* New York: The Free Press.

Reichheld, F. 2002. The one number you need to grow. *Harvard Business Review* (December), pp. 1–11.

Reidenbach, R. E., and R. W. Goeke. 2005. *Value-driven channel strategy: An extension of lean.* Quality Press.

Reidenbach, R. E., and R. W. Goeke. 2006. *Customer value and Six Sigma: Keys to sustainable differentiation.* Quality Press.

Rigby, D. K., F. Reichheld, and C. Dawson. 2003. Winning customer loyalty is the key to a winning CRM strategy. *Ivey Management Services* (March/April), London, Ontario.

The value of customer retention: A business without a customer retention plan will lose revenues and market share. 2005. Available online at www.marketingprinciples.com.

Walker Information Services. 2005. *Walker Loyalty Report for Communications Services.* Indianapolis, In: Author.

# Index

Entries in *ITALIC* indicate a figure entry

## A

Attribute-level analysis, *29*, 29–30
Appropriate monitoring system, 123;
        *See also* Monitoring plan
        effectiveness

## B

B2B; *See* Business-to-business (B2B)
Brand image, 14–15
Budgets, and forecasts, 105–108
Business information systems,
        monitoring plan
        effectiveness, 134
Business performance results, 134
Business-to-business (B2B), 36
Business-unit strategies, and
        product/market and corporate
        strategies, 151–152

## C

Challenge, 88
Challenger, 111
Cognitive measure, and customer
        value, 22
Competing for customers, 157–161
Competition
        and market segments, 53–62

planning for, 3–11
        where to compete, 49–62
Competitive decision making, *4*
Competitive market planning, 8–11
Competitive planning, 3–11; *See also*
        Planning; Competition
        context of, *158*
Competitive value analysis, 65–66
Competitive value matrix, 26–28, *27,
        66, 87*
Competitive value model, *24, 64*
Competitive value proposition, 81–97
        product/market objectives, 82–83
        product/market strategy, 84–97
Competitor vulnerability matrix,
        74–75, *75*
Consultants, reliability of, 142–143
Corporate champion, and plan
        deployment, 139
Corporate image, 14–15
Corporate strategies, and business-unit
        and product/market strategies,
        151–152
Corporate structure
        restructuring of, 152–154
        and strategy, 152–154
Corporate support, and plan
        deployment, 139
Corporate-level planning, 5–6
        growth strategies, *5*

CTQ/process matrix, and value-
strategy-process linkage,
115–117, *116*
Culture, managing change, 154–155
Culture change, managing of, 154–155
Current value proposition, 63–80, 159
competitive value analysis, 65–66
competitive value matrix, *66*
competitive value model, *64*
customer acquisition, 74–76
customer loyalty matrix, *77*, 77–78
customer retention, 76–80
driver-level analysis, 66–67
market opportunity identification,
70–74
value strengths and weaknesses,
66–70
value-driver summary, 64–65
VPC-level analysis, 67–70
Customer
competing for, 157–161
defections of, 36
importance of, 35–36
loss of, 36
and surveys, 141–142
Customer, understanding of, 144–145
Customer acquisition, 23, 74–76
attribute-level analysis, *29*, 29–30
competitive value matrix, 26–28
driver-level analysis, 28–29
value model, 24–26
vulnerability matrix, *31*, 31–33
Customer loyalty
assessing of, 39, 42
matrix, *41*, 42–46
matrix intervention, 42–46
programs for, 38–39
value model, *40*, 40
value of, 37–39
Customer loyalty matrix, *41*, 42–46,
*77*, 77–78
individual intervention, 42–46
systematic intervention, 42–46
Customer retention, 76–80
Customer satisfaction, and customer
value, 22
Customer surveys, 141–142
Customer value; *See also* Value
cognitive measure, 22

and customer satisfaction, 22
equals worth, 21–22
market based, 21–22
Customer value initiative,
technological view of value,
148–149
Customer value model, *40*, 40
Customer-focused value stream,
112–115

**D**

Dashboard overview, monitoring plan
effectiveness, 130–132
Data collection, monitoring plan
effectiveness, 127–129
Deployment
introduction to, 137–138
long-term keys, 147–155
short-term keys, 139–147
Diagnostic snapshots, monitoring plan
effectiveness, 132–134
Driver-level analysis, *28*, 28–29,
66–67

**E**

Employees, rewards for, 147

**F**

Focus, and competition, 50–62
Follower, 111
Following, 87–88
Forecasts, and budgets, 105–108

**G**

Gap analysis, 85

**H**

Head-to-head driver analysis, *67, 91*
Horizontal integration, 6

**I**

Image, 14–15
Intended value proposition, 9–11,
159–160
Internal performance matrix
monitoring plan effectiveness,
124–126

# K

Key milestones, 103

# L

Leader, 111
Lean initiatives
  and customer value initiatives,
    149–150
  and value-strategy-process linkage,
    117–121
Leveraging, 71–74
Loyalty; *See* Customer loyalty
Loyalty customer; *See* Customer loyalty

# M

Managing, market segments, 139–140
*Managing Customer Value,* 20
Market based, and value, 21–22
Market development, 5
Market opportunities, 70–74, 79
Market opportunity identification, 70–74
Market penetration, 5
Market segments, 52–53
  customer acquisition, 74–76
  customer retention, 76–80
  leveraging, 71–74
  measuring of, 139–140
  opportunity identification, 70–74
  product/market matrix, *51*, 52–62
  where to compete, 53–62
Marketing mix objectives, 99–103
Monitoring plan effectiveness
  business information systems, 134
  dashboard overview, 130–132
  data collection, 127–129
  diagnostic snapshots, 132–134
  internal performance matrix,
    124–126
  real-time reporting, 129–130
  responsiveness, 129
  transactional measures of customer
    value, 126–132
Multifunctional teams, utilization
  of, 146

# N

Niche, 88

# O

Opportunity identification, 70–74
Organizations
  restructuring, 152–154
  structure and strategy, 152–154

# P

Performance measure, 103
Plan performance reviews,
  150–151
Planning
  competitive decision making, 4
  context of competitive, *158*
  corporate-level, 5–6
  effective competitive, 3
  for competition, 3–11
  product/market-level, 7–11
  SBU, 3–5, 6–7
  levels and purposes, *50*
Price, 15
Product development, 5
Product lines, focus and competition,
  50–51
Product/market action programs,
  103–105, *104*
Product/market matrix, *51*, 52–62
Product/market objectives, 82–83
  assumptions, 83
Product/market strategy, 84–97
  and corporate and business-unit
    strategies, 151–152
  and marketing mix objectives,
    99–103
Product/market-level planning, 7–11

# Q

QTC level, and value-strategy-process
  linkage, 111–112
Qualifiers, 70–71
Questionnaires, 142

# R

Real-time reporting, monitoring plan
  effectiveness, 129–130
Recipient perceptions, 145
Research vendors, reliability of,
  142–143

Responsiveness, monitoring plan
    effectiveness, 129
Rewards, for employees, 147

## S

Satisfaction, and value, 18–20
SBU; *See* Strategic business unit (SBU)
Six sigma
    integration with customer value
        initiative, 149–150
    and value-strategy-process linkage,
        117–121
Sticky customers, 38–39
Strategic business unit (SBU), 3, 6–7
Strategic focus, 141
    and corporate structure, 152–154
Strategic measures, 18, 19, 141
Surveys, 141–142

## T

Tactical measures, 18, 19
Teams, utilization of, 146
Transactional measures of customer
    value
    dashboard overview, 130–132
    data collection, 127–129
    effectiveness of, 127
    monitoring plan effectiveness,
        126–132
    real-time reporting, 129–130
    responsiveness, 129
    survey, 127, *128*, 129
Transactional survey, 127, *128*, 129

## V

Value; *See also* Customer value
    calculation of, 15
    competitive proposition, 16
    comprehensive view of, *14*
    current proposition, 8–9, 63–80
    customer, 13–16
    defined, 13
    examples of, 15–16
    intended proposition, 9–11, 159–160

learned, 17
    market based, 21–22
    not satisfaction, 18–20
    product and market specific, 16–17
    and profitability, 20
    properties of, 16–18
    relativity of, 16
Value gaps, and value-strategy-process
    linkage, 111–112
Value model, 24–25
    managerial component, 25
    predictive component, 25
Value opportunity identification
    matrix, *71, 89*
Value performance criteria; *See* VPC-
    level analysis
Value performance criteria gaps, *114*
Value proposition management,
    99–108
    budgets and forecasts, 105–108
    marketing mix objectives, 99–103
    product/market action programs,
        103–105
Value propositions, managing of,
    99–108
Value stream, and value-strategy-
    process linkage, 112–115
Value-driver summary, 64–65
Value-strategy-process linkage,
    109–121, *110*
    calculate critical value gaps,
        111–112
    CTQ/process matrix, 115–117
    identify the key value stream,
        112–115
    lean initiatives, 117–121
    six sigma, 117–121
Vertical integration, 6
VPC-level analysis, 67–70
Vulnerability matrix, *31,* 31–33

## W

Worth it, 21–22